UFO RETRIEVALS

THE RECOVERY OF ALIEN SPACECRAFT

JENNY RANDLES

BLANDFORD

This book is dedicated to Dr J. Allen Hynek and Leonard Stringfield, two true pioneers, original thinkers and dedicated researchers whom it has been my privilege to know.

A BLANDFORD BOOK

First published in the UK by Blandford
A Cassell Imprint
Cassell plc, Wellington House,
125 Strand, London WC2R 0BB

Reprinted 1995 (twice), 1996 (twice)

Distributed in the United States by Sterling Publishing Co., Inc., 387 Park Avenue South, New York, NY 10016-8810

Distributed in Australia by Capricorn Link (Australia) Pty Ltd 2/13 Carrington Road, Castle Hill, NSW 2154

British Library Cataloguing-in-Publication Data
A catalogue entry for this title is available from the British Library

ISBN 0–7137–2493–5

Typeset by Method Limited, Epping, Essex, UK

Printed and bound in Great Britain by
Mackays of Chatham PLC, Chatham, Kent

CONTENTS

THE GREATEST STORY NEVER TOLD

I live each day in a world filled with UFOs and weird close encounters. This can be a very harrowing experience. Time and again, I hear stories – channelled through from some bored newspaper office, via a scientific institute wishing to remain aloof, or just by word of mouth from housewives and factory workers. A witness will begin cautiously, testing the water, saying nervously: 'You're probably not going to believe this, but . . .' Then gradually the person unburdens something that has haunted them for years – telling of that one brief moment when they touched the deepest mystery in the universe.

I am not surprised by people's reluctance to talk. They cannot know if I am about to giggle uncontrollably or to report their tale to the CIA.

These bizarre stories come in many forms. A man researching aviation history in the UK writes to me from Cumbria, telling me that in 1990 he met a young American woman photographer then working for the Defense Department in Washington. She wanted to tell him about the day she was asked to take pictures in a secret hangar on an air base where she was shown 16 bodies of dead aliens. Bits taken from crashed UFOs hung on the hangar's walls. The truth about the aliens and UFOs was to be made public, the woman had insisted, probably in 1992.

It was 1993 when the aviation historian contacted me, soliciting my help on another matter and mentioning this only in passing. The world is still waiting for the news release . . .

'Friend of a friend'-type anecdotes rub shoulders in my mail with more serious authoritative-sounding, yet absurd, data. For instance, a carefully referenced dossier, entitled 'The Secret Government', arrived in 1990, seemingly from a certain Milton Cooper. It claimed to be a concise history of the US government's dealings with an alien race, following the capture of hardware in 1947. Taken on its own, this treatise might just as well have been written by the late British comedian Tommy Cooper, as by the earnest researcher Milton. It had about as much credibility for me, since it was full of secret pacts, abduction nightmares, and terrible experiments on human beings. The whole document was anathema to an objective, neo-sceptical investigator; I doubted the existence of aliens, let alone that a group of them could get captured by the US government and be hidden away from the world for half a century.

Of course, by 1990 I knew that Milton Cooper's work was not to be taken on its own. It was part of a UFO sub-culture that was sweeping the USA; it was just as believable as anything else that was appearing then. I argued vociferously against its implications; indeed, so vociferously that I actually got sued by one US ufologist who disliked my naturally sceptical tone about some of the evidence. Whether I was right or wrong to be so disbelieving is not important. What matters is that when material like Cooper's undoubtedly sincere thesis reached my door, my gut reaction was certainly not to cry 'whoopee' and call the highest paying news source; instead, it was to be properly cautious and wait to see if someone, somewhere, was going to confirm it. Failing that, I would make up my own mind whether to believe it or not.

Then a letter arrived from Lieutenant-Colonel Robert Bowker of the US Air Force (USAF). He had first met alien technology in 1950 while flying from Wake Island to Honolulu. 'Red lights in a pattern came up on the port side and spun the medium-frequency ADF [on-board electronic navigational equipment] so fast, I thought it would be destroyed, and turned it off.' Soon after, Bowker had to comfort a pilot of a C–54 inbound from Wake to Hickam Air Force Base on the island of Oahu. He was 'so shook up I had to help him hold his whisky glass'. Eight objects had shot straight at him, closing at 1,000 mph. Just before impact, four had passed above and four below his aircraft. Both the C–54 pilot and Bowker were warned by an NSA [security] officer to remain silent about this top-secret encounter. Bowker was pretty sure that he now knew what UFOs were and that those officers in the 28 security levels *above* 'top secret' – the one to which he had been officially cleared – were in possession of a lot more data about UFOs.

Some of the people who contact me connect UFOs with more sinister motivations. Steve from Washington D.C. wrote to tell me that a massive 'think tank' was in operation that practised 'psychotronic warfare' on people. By this he meant that electronic devices of extreme sophistication and secrecy were being used on human beings to adapt their psychology and to get them to see weird things or act in a certain way. It was terrifying. Steve reeled off project code-names and reported about how UFOs were all intermixed with these devious experiments. He added, 'I think some very shady things are going on in the black hole of the Pentagon's "black budget" ' – which, given the history of this planet and humanity's penchant for developing ever more horrible things to do to one another, I do not find hard to believe. That said, I am not quite sure I would go so far as to think that UFOs are what another writer has termed a 'propaganda myth', designed to deflect attention away from the Pentagon's nefarious research operations.

But, then again, after spending four years researching the alleged UFO crash in Rendlesham Forest, East Anglia (see pages 131–148), I had begun to suspect that something more terrestrial and nasty might have lain behind the secrets of that case. Later, out of the blue, I got a call from a British scientist who said that he specialized in nuclear physics and rocketry. (I checked him out, and he was just who he said he was.) He told me that he had been piqued by certain references in my investigation and, on probing the matter further, he had discovered the awesome truth. Something devastating, but non-alien in nature, had indeed taken place within that forest. However, he stressed that he was going to do nothing because, as he graphically phrased it, when you start sniffing around ultra-sensitive issues such as these, you are 'messing with something for which you can end up at the bottom of the Thames'. Incredible, certainly; unbelievable, probably. Yet typical of the kind of thing that I was hearing day in and day out about the so-called massive conspiracy of silence that surrounds the UFO mystery.

Quite a collection of people – anonymous tale-tellers, government agents, air force officers – have written to me; it makes you think. But if you have any trouble believing their stories, you might find one more communicant rather more credible. He was about as big a name as you can get. I think anyone would be convinced by Lord Peter Hill-Norton. No wide-eyed mystic, he had been a UK Admiral of the Fleet and former head of the entire UK Ministry of Defence. If he was talking nonsense, then we would have to start worrying seriously about the security of the free world. Of course, it all depends on what you define as nonsense. When, in August 1992, he expressed his sincere opinions about my research into the Rendlesham Forest crash, he was doing so from a position of informed judgement. If he had been talking instead about military matters, world politics or

6

security implications, we would not dare question his opinion. We would welcome and respect it. In truth, when Lord Hill-Norton expressed his view of the UFO cover-up of an alleged incident he probably *was* talking about all of these things. He stated that my summary of the alien hypothesis behind the case was 'fair and convincing' and, he added, 'as I said to Lord Trefgarne, either something landed in our airspace, or the [USAF] Colonel and his merry men at an operational USAF base in Britain were hallucinating . . . if this is not of defence interest then it certainly should be.' I should point out that he certainly did not believe that these officers were hallucinating, and nor do I.

However, after 20 years amidst this alien reality, the truth behind these assorted claims remains shrouded in confusion. No matter how forcefully a witness may tell their tale, and no matter what explanation they think must apply, the answer eludes our grasp. Nobody knows what is actually going on here; not the witnesses, not the media, and certainly not the authorities.

Or do they?

The idea that the authorities *do* know the truth is, in a sense, the greatest story *never* told – the terrifying reality that supposedly underpins everything extraterrestrial, from vague lights flitting about the night-time sky to spectacular sightings that make lurid headlines in the tabloid Press. It says that an alien intelligence is here on our planet, toying with us, laughing at our defences. Worse still, that the powers that be know this as a fact beyond any possible dispute – just as they have known it for half a century; they are merely unwilling to come clean and say so. There is a simple reason why they know, the story goes. You see, once, long ago (and perhaps several other times since), the leaders of this world captured the indisputable proof: they got bits of a spaceship, or even an entire machine. In some versions of the story, they also procured alien pilots, both alive and dead, and then performed stunning autopsies on them. This shocking, yet profound, reality is being withheld from public awareness for reasons that someone, somewhere, has decreed to surpass our world-wide and seemingly self-evident right to know. Yet, it is also a cover-up that is fast eroding; the truth is emerging bit by bit. Major books, such as Tim Good's *Alien Liaison*, have professed this in bold letters from the lofty heights of the best-seller lists.

The unexpected success of these books has been noted by

the Establishment media, who have even written articles quizzing what they term 'respectable' publishers about how they can allow such nonsense to be released. Is it just a con trick to make the publishers money, they wonder? Well, no; that is, generally speaking, not the case. These books are sincere in their purpose and specific in their aims. Whether they do tell the truth, or are infused with speculation dressed up as reality and fuelled by tall tales that masquerade as fact, is something that must be judged by their individual merits. But they are genuine in their motivation and they illustrate just how strongly this belief finds its mark in today's society.

We are desperate not to be alone within the vastness of the universe. Yet, of course, we must temper that understandable desperation with cool rationality: wanting something to be true is far removed from it actually being true. We still can only wonder when we face this huge question: Can these incredible claims possibly be real? That, in simple terms, is what this book sets out to determine.

I have compiled a chronological account of 32 cases during the past hundred years, most of them being post-World War 2. In these reports it is alleged that something strange crashed out of the sky. Moreover, it also usually inferred by some that this object was a UFO (for which read extraterrestrial spacecraft) which, of course, may also have been piloted. In quite a few of these cases, some kind of military involvement is described where the purpose might arguably have been the recovery of this wreckage and/or any alien pilots who happened to accompany it.

For over 20 years a small body of UFO researchers has attempted to collect evidence of this kind. The pioneer was American Leonard Stringfield, who coined the term 'retrievals' for these reputed operations. I have had the good fortune to meet Len, whom I consider a fine researcher, an unsung hero of the UFO world and a very nice man as well. He deserves real credit for legitimizing a field which, even in the wacky world of UFOs, long seemed for many of us to be simply too absurd.

By far the greatest amount of attention has been focused upon the Roswell, New Mexico, retrieval of July 1947. Half-a-dozen books have appeared and two movies are on the drawing board (one which reportedly involves Steven Spielberg). Ufologists often term this the most important case in world history, although it also has plenty of critics. Aside from the events near RAF Bentwaters in Suffolk, England, in December

1980 (which has also caught the attention of the UFO world in a fairly big way), many of the other investigations are little known. This seemed an appropriate time to review them all together.

I should emphasize that I have no particular belief to vindicate. While I feel, generally, that there is *something* interesting within some parts of the UFO evidence, I also realize, after so many years as an investigator, that the *majority* of evidence is peppered with misperception, mistaken identity and a pinch of fabrication. This means that I will try to be objective and present the good, the bad and the occasionally downright ugly when it comes to assessing the facts behind any specific case.

Sometimes, as you will see, we will be forced to conclude that a crash simply never happened. Other times, it may be apparent that the events were real but their extraterrestrial relevance is non-existent. Yet on other occasions we may have to balance our judgement and remain indecisive. However, in a few instances, there is a *prima facie* case that seems to support the claims of the UFO contingent. If we find such a case, I will say so. But if the sceptics make a telling argument and offer a simpler explanation, I will also describe what that is and why it seems to work.

The ultimate conclusion will be down to you. It is your task to sift the evidence for these alleged retrievals and decide what, if anything, did crash and whether anything at all was ever retrieved. Then – if you feel up to it – you can face the final great challenge. Ask yourself just how close we have come to real proof that the aliens have landed (albeit sometimes with a bit of a bump), or, indeed, that someone in the darkened corridors of power knows this awesome fact to be true. Then, if you answer these questions in the affirmative, ponder the devastating implications that they would have.

Jenny Randles
Fleetwood, England

CHAPTER ONE

RETRIEVALS –
THE EARLY YEARS

Rather surprisingly, alleged crashes by alien spacecraft are not simply a modern-day phenomenon. As the reports in this section will show, there are over a century of documented claims for us to investigate. While many of these early tales will prove to be rather dubious, that actually provides a useful insight: we can assess the motives behind, and the social reactions to, what were always rather amazing stories and apply that thought to more current episodes, which are often judged to be more credible.

The one thing that all these early cases have in common is that they predate the very first sighting of what was recognized as a UFO – or rather a 'flying saucer', as it was termed by one enterprising journalist. That watershed came on 24 June 1947 and marked the beginning of the modern belief in alien intruders. The following cases come from a time when extraterrestrials were merely the product of fanciful novels by Jules Verne and H.G. Wells and the days of tabloid newspapers, mass TV coverage and Hollywood space movies were part of a distant future age. It will be fascinating to see what difference all this makes.

1871
THE CABINET-MAKER AND THE SPACESHIP

In 1979, David Langford, a Berkshire physicist, published a small treatise under 100 pages long. It was titled, in a fashion that matches its verbiage, 'An account of a meeting with denizens of another world, 1871'.

That archaic phrase reputedly came from an original manuscript that one William Loosley had written in the 1870s which had been discovered by one of his descendants about a century later. In his preface to the book, Langford termed it either 'the product of a remarkable imagination or alterna-

tively [it] could almost fully justify [William Loosley's] title.'
Loosley, according to Langford, was a cabinet-maker in High
Wycombe, Buckinghamshire who died in 1893. His story ('written in a fever', according to a note scrawled upon it by his
wife) supposedly described an encounter on 3 October 1871
with a crash-landed spaceship. Langford lovingly reproduces
this account and then adds 50 pages of rambling commentary
about its possible interpretation.

The 'noisy star' plunged from the sky over Plummers Hill,
according to Loosley's amusing prose. Never a writer who
would use one word when a dozen more can spring to mind, the
cabinet-maker described his close encounter with a small squat
object that extruded some kind of sensor and probed his body.
On the ground where it had crashed to earth, 'the grass and
weeds lay bent and slightly flattened, showing where they had
been pressed down over a wide expanse – I judged it circular . . .'. He was then allowed to witness a kind of moving
picture show of alien images, some of which seemed to presage
future technology and cosmological knowledge not imagined
during the 1870s. Eventually, the reluctant contactee fled, hiding his secret in a compartment locked for years inside one of
his cabinet's drawers. There is no doubt that Langford presents
a wonderful tale worthy of our attention and one which fits
well with later UFO discoveries, as he himself seems well
aware. The 'abduction' scenario recounted by Loosley is typical of many that have followed since.

The Loosleys were a real family, actually related to David
Langford (although he does not make this clear in his text). No
doubt William Loosley's biography could be checked out and
found to be accurate.

Note the flattened circle, which, in 1979, was nearly a year
too early for the first publicized examples of so-called 'crop circles'. Some of these, experts were later not slow to realize,
occurred in the High Wycombe area. Indeed, by the 1970s this
was known to be a mini 'hot spot' for UFO activity, with several good examples of strange lights and cars stopped by mysterious energies.

When Langford's book was reviewed by the UFO press
from 1980 onwards, it was treated rather interestingly. Some
sources, notably in the USA, were willing to embrace it as an
example of a pre-flying-saucer-age UFO. Others, including
several British magazines, were much more sceptical.

Janet and Colin Bord, reviewing the book in *Fortean*

Times in 1980, pointed out that Langford went to some lengths to chart Loosley's background, including photographs of him, his family, their shop and even his gravestone. What he made no attempt to do was illustrate the extraordinary book for itself, which was, to say the least, a rather curious omission.

Langford does state that the 'manuscript of William Robert Loosley is clearly not a fabrication on his part', citing how it refers to science then well beyond the man's knowledge. As to it being a subsequent hoax (i.e. post-dating Loosley's death), the author merely notes: 'I can only declare that the manuscript has so far withstood every test of authenticity to which it has been subjected.' However, nothing is said about what these tests were, who actually carried them out, when they occurred, or even what was concluded.

As you may have surmised, this is not a genuine UFO crash. It is, in fact, an audacious hoax and, for once, the hoaxer is known. The entire story was the product of David Langford himself, partly as a spoof and partly to test the reactions of UFO enthusiasts. He told *UFO Brigantia* magazine in July 1990 that his editor, Paul Barnett, at the British publishers David & Charles (then noted largely for sedate books about transport) gave him a brief to 'write a spoof book [and] examine the evidence as a physicist would . . . [while making it] sufficiently over the top that no close reader could believe it.' And so he did precisely that (and I have checked it all out with Paul Barnett). There are obvious clues, such as the lack of documentation discussed above. The fact that Langford's biography lists him as a successful science-fiction writer is another point that might have been borne in mind, but hardly ever was. To be sure, the author did try to discredit his own work by over-exuberance, but perhaps he tried too hard.

Langford was also delighted by how some people read into his statement about the testing of the manuscript that it had, in fact, been successfully validated by modern-day researchers. However, if you read carefully what Langford says, he claims nothing of the sort. His wording does not preclude the possibility that the number of tests to which this manuscript was subjected was actually nil – and that was exactly how many tests it was given, because the manuscript never existed in the first place. Not one media source or UFO expert, including those who were convinced by the tale, tracked the writer down and asked to see this precious evidence.

David Langford's quirky sense of humour would easily be

discovered by anybody who checked him out via his books or columns in computer magazines. He even admitted the truth after his text went out of print. He did so in fairly prominent places: for example, *New Scientist* magazine in 1988. Even so, few saw the truth through their own desire to believe.

Crop-circle researchers also seized upon his tale. The flattened circle owed nothing to these modern phenomena and everything to UFO stories of 'landing nests', which themselves may well have triggered some of the crop circle hoaxers into action. Yet, at least one noted 'cereologist' took the Loosley story seriously. Indeed, it also appeared, without criticism, in two of the top-selling UFO-related books of the 1980s and early 1990s.

There are obvious lessons to be learnt from this episode. Never take anything as proven without first attempting to authenticate it directly. Just because it does not seem on the surface to be a hoax and its original author is not obviously making money from it, it does not mean that somebody else lurking in the background might not be. In any case, as here, there can be many – often obscure – motives for trickery.

1884:
NUGGETS OVER NEBRASKA

This case was unearthed by Jerome Clark, one of the leading experts in the 'airship waves' of the late nineteenth century. People all over the American West and Midwest claimed to have seen wondrous winged vehicles sailing through the air and the newspapers were full of their appearances. This particular tale preludes all of those accounts by ten years, which enhances its interest. It first saw publication in the *Nebraska Nugget* in June 1884, but it has resurfaced several times since.

Reputedly, on 6 June 1884, in a remote area of southern Nebraska called Dundy County, a blazing object fell from the sky, making a terrible whirring sound as it did so. Cowhands who rushed to the scene found cog-wheels and other bits of debris scattered on the ground. There was scorched grass surrounding the wreckage and intense heat. One of the eyewitnesses collapsed after having got too close and suffered skin burns and singed hair.

Over the next couple of days, many locals went to see the

object, even though the metal fragments still glowed with heat and the sand around it was fused like glass. After a while, when it was approachable, some of the metal wheels and other shapes were lifted. They seemed to be made out of something like brass but much lighter. This interesting characteristic of UFO wreckage featured 60 years later in the most famous crash incident of all – the Roswell affair in New Mexico.

The story was carried by the *Daily State Journal* in Lincoln, the Nebraska state capital, on 8 June. It was the first to suggest an extraterrestrial origin, noting that this seemed the only likely source for the fallen object if the incident were being truthfully related and not subject to wild exaggeration.

Clark notes that on 10 June the same Lincoln paper carried a further (more jokey) report in which the wreckage was said to have vanished before onlookers, just like a spoonful of salt dissolving in water. Indeed, as the researcher points out, this rather suggests that a spoonful of salt was exactly what the writer expected you to take with this entire story. By 11 June, the editorial section of the *State Journal* was writing the whole thing off in even more flippant terms, although no source for a hoax was ever established or admitted to, it would appear.

In 1964, when the story was republished in Omaha, a member of the Dundy Historical society checked it out by interviewing people from the area who had been children in the late 1800s. None of them could recall anything about the incident and, of course, no such area of fused ground or trace of the wreckage itself has ever been found to support the authenticity of this crash. It is unlikely one can blame such a disappearance on a Victorian style government cover-up. More probably the events simply never happened.

1897
A SPACEMAN BURIED IN THE WILD WEST

During the airship wave of 1896–97, there were several more reports of alleged crashes by these flying devices. However, most of them were obvious yarns spun by newspapers to better stories in print in rivals.

The one case that has intrigued ever since, and indeed has even spawned a movie based upon it, is the alleged incident at

Aurora, Texas, where an alien body is still thought by some to be buried. The first reports were published in the *Dallas Morning News* of 19 April 1897, towards the end of the airship wave and after countless other stories about these floating craft had been told. By then, a tale needed to be pretty special to command much attention, and this one certainly was.

A man called S.E. Haydon reported that at 6 am on 17 April an airship had appeared over the small town of Aurora, about 70 km (45 miles) north of Dallas. In apparent trouble, it struck the tower of a windmill owned by the local judge and scattered wreckage over the flowerbeds. A badly maimed body was recovered and supposedly pronounced non-human by one T.J. Weems, said to be a local signals officer and astronomy buff. Some material in the wreckage had hieroglyphic symbols on it – interestingly another feature that was to crop up half a century later at Roswell.

In 1966 researchers, who were beginning to piece together the story of the long-forgotten airship wave, became intrigued by this case and began to dig into it. Some supportive evidence was uncovered, notably that the named judge had indeed lived in Aurora at the time. However, little else came to light to back up the incident and many local citizens flatly denied that it was true, pointing out that local histories written only a few years after the supposed event never even mentioned it. Had it really occurred, this seems difficult to understand. In addition, it was learnt that T.J. Weems did exist but that he was, in fact, a blacksmith, not a military officer as alleged, which might cast doubt on the accuracy of the rest of the story.

One ufologist was determined to get to the truth. He was Hayden Hewes of the International UFO Bureau. Between 1972 and 1974 he and his team made a determined effort to prove that the crash had really occurred and that, as mentioned in the original story (which produced no sequel reports in the Press at the time), the dead alien aeronaut was buried in Aurora's cemetery. The Bureau had the help of the *Dallas Times Herald*, which promoted the investigation and helped trace many points of information. Eileen Buckle, writing for *FSR* (*Flying Saucer Review*) magazine in 1973, referred to a *Herald* article, published on 1 June 1973, in which the paper appeared to have established first-hand proof. The paper describes three eyewitnesses who professed knowledge of the incident. Notably, 98-year-old G.C. Curley from Lewisville was quoted from his nursing home as saying how two friends had ridden over to Aurora and come back to describe the airship. It had hit something near the judge's well and the 'alien' pilot was 'badly torn up' and beyond description. As for the metal fragments, the friends said there was nothing like them on earth at the time.

A 91-year-old woman, Mary Evans, also told of what she saw. She had forgotten all about it for over 70 years, but could now recall the excitement in the town and how her parents forbade her to go to the crash site. Her mother and father did go, however, and told how the ship had exploded but the remains of its alien pilot were gathered and buried in a grave. The only new detail, she added, was that the pilot was small. However, Hayden Hewes notes that when he later spoke to Mrs Evans, she was to claim, in apparent contradiction, 'I didn't say it this way.' And worse still, Hewes says that G.C. Curley, when traced, turned out to be actually called A.J. McCurley and he was in Oklahoma at the time of the crash.

The media also reported on the UFO Bureau's alleged desire to dig up the grave and exhume the body. In response, the Aurora Cemetery Association took legal action against the ufologists, slapping an injunction on any such plan. In fact, the Bureau had not decided upon any such course of action, but were merely exploring the possibility. Later the cemetery association indicated that if there was what they termed an 'overwhelming probability' of finding an alien body in the graveyard, then they would probably support an exhumation. On 18 March 1974, when the ufologists attempted to get such permission, they were flatly denied. Instead, they were told that the cemetery association would use 'whatever means are available' to prevent the grave being opened.

As a result, the ufologists began to consider using sophisticated radar devices to scan the ground. As far as I know, this has never been done. Reference was made to the finding of fragments of odd metals at the site. These were analysed, according to the *Dallas Herald*, by Dr Tom Gray, a physicist at North Texas State University. They were recovered from the farm of Brawley Oates who, in the 1970s, owned the spot where the judge had lived 80 years previously (i.e. where the crash reputedly took place). The fragments were dug up by a student and another lecturer at the university after a scan by metal detectors. The pieces are said to have contained 75 per cent iron and 25 per cent zinc, plus some rarer trace elements. In the late nineteenth century, scientists lacked the knowledge to produce this unnatural combination of elements, so it could not have been produced on earth. However, by the middle of the following century it would have been possible, since the know-how was available. Although Dr Gray was quoted as saying that 'its physics stir my curiosity as a scientist', he insisted that he did not mean to imply the metal was extraterrestrial.

Hewes insisted that the research by his team could neither prove nor disprove the crash claims, but that he felt the case was important, because it offered the best hope of authenticating any of the airship-wave stories.

However, the Aurora town council itself was unconvinced. It told one British ufologist in 1972 that 'the entire event was a hoax', adding that this conclusion was reached on the lack of any hard evidence to support the claim – for example, records at the cemetery or recollection by any local residents in the town who survived from 1897 to 1972. The town council concluded that, in its view, the incident was a fabrication dreamt up by bored members of the local railway telegraphy office in the wake of previous tall tales spun all over the Midwest that spring, often by other railway workers.

Jerry Clark agrees, in principle. He shows that the story in the original Dallas paper has to be seen in context with its airship stories printed both before and after the Aurora affair. These told of ships spouting fire like Chinese dragons and three airship pilots who were spotted singing 'Nearer my God to thee!' These, he feels, hardly suggest credibility for any of the spate of stories being published that month.

In addition, Dr J. Allen Hynek – ex-scientific consultant to the US Air Force on UFO matters and, in 1973, founder of the Center for UFO Studies, now one of the most respected UFO groups in the world – had sent an investigator, William Driskell, to Aurora in 1966. Driskell had effectively killed off the story. He had learnt that there never had been a windmill at the site, that few other facts even began to check out and that the most likely solution was that the story was an attempt to revive the fortunes of Aurora after the diversion of the railways had threatened its future prosperity. If it was, it failed, for the town continued to decline.

The movie of the saga appeared in 1985 as *Aurora Encounter* and it has a quaint, almost home video, feel to it. It is hardly *Close Encounters of the Third Kind*, nevertheless it relates the 'events' with sprinklings of B-movie imagination.

However, it failed to revive interest in the case and, after the local courts insisted that the grave would never be exhumed, the Aurora spaceman faded into what is almost certain to be deserved obscurity.

1908:
THE SIBERIAN SPACEFALL

Apart from the Roswell affair or the Rendlesham Forest incidents, this classic episode is probably the most famous alleged UFO crash of all time. It is one of those few important instances where there is no question that something did crash: there is overwhelming physical evidence to support that fact; all that remains in dispute is what that something was. There are many die-hards who cling to the opinion that it was an alien space vessel, but that is certainly not the view shared by scientists, who have their own, more mundane, but no less spectacular, explanations for what caused the biggest peace-time explosion of the twentieth century.

It happened at about 7.07 am on 30 June 1908 near the Lower Tunguska River, which is within the vast, remote and inhospitable terrain of the central Siberian taiga (a huge area of forested land which is frozen in winter and swampy in summer; beneath the topsoil it is permafrost: earth which is frozen throughout the year). There was never any doubt that something awesome had occurred. The explosion was so huge that it caused damage nearly 650 km (400 miles) from the impact point (it was heard even further away), and the well-measured shock wave circled the earth twice. The column of fire projected into the air was witnessed far from the Tunguska region and the heat wave that spread out was felt hundreds of kilometres beyond the crash zone. For several nights all over northern Europe, the sky glowed sufficiently to read newspapers in London and to take photographs at midnight in Moscow. These effects were the result of huge clouds of dust thrown up into the atmosphere by the catastrophic impact. The assumption as to what had happened that summer's morning seemed simple: it was thought to be a medium to large-sized meteorite impact.

Astronomers knew that small balls of rock and microscopic specks of dust descended into the earth's atmosphere in

18

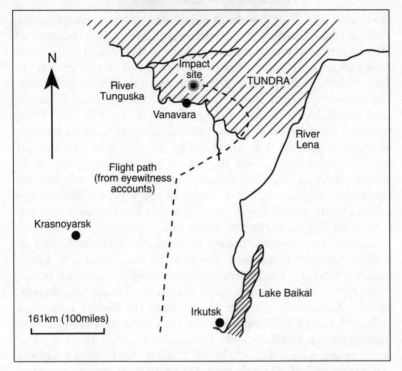

A map showing the location of the Siberian crash and object flightpath in 1908.

their thousands every day. They create flickers of light in the sky as the friction of re-entry burns them to a frazzle. Some larger ones, perhaps nearly a metre across, can produce a much more visual display and flare across the sky for several seconds. These are known as fireball meteors, or bolides. However, every now and then the rock is just too big or made of resistant fragments, like iron ore, to burn up. Then chunks do reach the earth. Several meteorite impacts a year are known, most falling harmlessly into the oceans or far from civilization.

Once in a while a truly big meteor – perhaps a hundred metres or so in diameter – gets through the atmosphere. When it hits the ground, a massive crater results, like the spectacular one near Winslow in Arizona. About 1.6 km (1 mile) wide, it draws tourists from all over the world. The impact that created this dent occurred tens of thousands of years ago.

Scientists also know that every few million years a gigantic meteor or, indeed, an asteroid (which are like vast meteors

19

that circle the solar system in permanent orbit) must strike the earth's atmosphere. One of these plunged into the gaseous atmosphere of the planet Jupiter in July 1994. Such a rock may be up to several kilometres in diameter and it will inevitably make its way to the earth's surface more or less in one piece. The consequences of this, whether impacting on land or in the sea, would be truly devastating. There is mounting evidence that one such collision around 63 million years ago rocked the earth so violently that all the dust blocked out the sun for many months and killed off whole species, including most dinosaurs. A similar, enormous meteorite strike will happen again, but we do not know when; it could be tomorrow or a million years from now. However, we do know that whenever it hits, all life on earth will be at risk.

Given the political unrest in Russia and the difficulty of getting into the taiga near the turn of the century, it was a long time before a scientific expedition went in search of the meteorite that had fallen near the River Tunguska. In fact, Leonid Kulik only got permission from the Soviet regime in 1921 and it was 1927 before he had the time and resources to undertake the arduous trek. He finally reached the centre of destruction, which was 800 km (500 miles) north of the nearest large town (Irkutsk) and over 1,200 km (800 miles) north-east of the city of Novosibirsk. Search as he might, Kulik could not find any pieces of meteorite. Given the enormous nature of the explosion evident all around him, this was puzzling. The rock must have been at least 30 m (100 ft) in diameter. It could not possibly have all vaporized. Yet there was no trace at all of meteoritic debris.

Moreover, there was another problem. When Kulik carefully mapped the circle of devastation – trees felled like pins in a bowling alley, others stripped bare of bark, signs of fire hundreds of square kilometres around him – he realized that at the centre point of the impact there was an area of trees still standing in a swamp. The trees had been subjected to powerful shock waves which had ripped off all their branches, but they had not been flattened.

Kulik guessed that the remains of the meteor were buried in the swamp at the centre of the impact zone. It was 20 years before geophysical surveys were to prove him wrong. The swamp had been there for tens of thousands of years. It had not been disturbed by an explosion in 1908 which had left a crater to be filled in by permafrost during the years between the explosion and Kulik's first visit to the site. Indeed, the surveys proved that there simply was no impact crater in the taiga at all.

There seemed only one possible conclusion from this startling evidence: the object was not a meteor; nothing had impacted on the ground. The explosion had been in the air above the forest and the shock-wave energy had fanned downwards and outwards. The immediate area underneath the exploding body had been shielded from the outward thrust. Precisely what sort of explosion could have caused such devastation was now the basis of intense discussion. As air travel and roads improved, scientists flocked to the Tunguska River region, bent on learning more. These explorations continue to this day.

Post-World War 2, aerial photos of the destruction of Hiroshima and Nagasaki were compared with photos of the flattened Siberian taiga. They were stunningly similar. It took less then six months for someone to draw the obvious conclusion. A. Kasantsev, a science-fiction author, published a short story in January 1946 in which he offered serious speculation that an alien spacecraft powered by nuclear motors had blown up above Tunguska. He was rebuked by scientists for this nonsense; most of them still stood by the rapidly disintegrating theory of meteor impact. Further visits during the 1950s accrued some data that supported Kasantsev's audacious idea. Unfortunately, they were compromised by Soviet nuclear testing. This meant that the discovery of excess levels of caesium 137, a radioactive element, might have had a more recent origin than dating back to the 1908 explosion.

One important experiment, carried out in 1959, demonstrated, by way of scale models and hovering explosive charges, that the damage on the ground could only have resulted from an impact about 5 km (3 miles) above the surface. This finally killed off the meteorite hypothesis. As a result, scientists began to consider a small comet, perhaps 150 m (500 ft) in diameter. Since comets are mostly composed of vaporizing ice from a small solid core, they would probably be more readily destroyed during passage through the earth's atmosphere. The chances of the earth being struck by a comet were much less than by a meteorite, simply because there are thought to be far fewer comets. Nevertheless, there are certainly enough of them to make this a likelihood every few millennia and, if the comet were small enough, it might not have been seen on its way towards the earth. This, in fact, was the main argument raised against the theory. Most felt that astronomers would have spotted the comet and plotted its progress, rather than be taken by surprise with the 1908 event just as everybody else had been. The comet theory would successfully explain the dust clouds – from the vaporized debris. This fits the 'black rain' that local people described falling on them afterwards and the green clouds seen in the sky.

There is no doubt that most scientists today prefer the small comet theory. Ufologist Kevin Randle (later to achieve fame in connection with the Roswell crash story) interviewed one of America's best-loved astronomers, Dr James Van Allen, in 1977. Van Allen (who discovered the radiation belts encircling the earth) said quite explicitly, 'I think there is nothing that I have heard about the evidence which excludes a comet as the most reasonable possibility.' But he did add, very fairly, that if clear evidence of radioactivity were uncovered from the site, then things might be different. Suggestions about this radioactivity have appeared occasionally. In 1965, for example, it was first discovered that trees within the impact zone were experiencing accelerated growth. The effects were noticeably similar to studies of plant regrowth on Bikini atoll after the nuclear detonation there in 1958. In 1965 it was thought to be evidence for alterations to the genetic structure of the trees within the Tunguska region, presumably caused by residual radiation; it has since been noted in other areas following huge explosions. For example, it was seen in the vicinity of Mount St Helens in the USA, which erupted in 1980. More interesting was the report in *Nature* magazine in 1965 that the examination of the rings on tree bark in the USA indicated evidence of the deposition of nuclear material in the year following the 1908 event. If verified, this is hard to equate with any known natural cause.

As a result of these findings, a few scientists, such as geophysicist A.V. Zolotov, have endeavoured to find a compromise. Not wishing to argue that an alien spacecraft could have flown over Siberia in 1908, he has sought a possible natural source for a nuclear explosion. No such thing is known to present-day science, which is not to say that none exists, of course; they may simply not yet have been found. Theories such as tiny black holes, pockets of anti-matter and the like have thus been postulated, but all are speculative, without support from mainstream science.

On the more avant-garde front, British science-fiction writer Ian Watson has penned a fascinating theory in his clever 1981 novel *Chekhov's Journey*. This combines writer Chekhov's real-life journey through Siberia in 1890 with the use of regression and progression hypnosis on actors and the idea that the Tunguska impact was caused by a man-made spacecraft. You might wonder how Watson's idea works when we obviously did not have spacecraft in 1908, but that is forgetting Einstein and Lorentz's research into the nature of space-time and relativity. Objects travelling fast enough can theoretically move from the future into the past!

The allure of the Siberian explosion being caused by a spacecraft (be it man-made or, perhaps more plausibly, a visiting vehicle from another planet) is still as strong as ever. While it has no overriding evidence to persuade us of its validity and it is rejected by almost all scientific commentators, they, themselves, have not proven the comet origin of the explosion. And there are still some problems with that theory. For instance, Kulik reported no evidence of radiation sickness from any of the local people who had witnessed the event. But his trips were in the 1920s and 1930s, before radiation sickness was recognized. According to Baxter and Atkins, describing later interviews with locals, some did refer to 'a strange disease' which might have been consistent with mild radiation sickness. Many reindeer were also found burnt to a crisp far from the impact point, although whether this was caused by thermal or nuclear energy is hard to conclude.

Several things are interesting from the eyewitnesses' testimonies. Many spoke of an oval-shaped mass moving across the sky. This implies a glowing spaceship more than a comet. The explosion is also described in terms very reminiscent of a nuclear mushroom cloud. Furthermore, several witnesses spoke of how the object changed course, as if desperately trying to make last-minute adjustments before it blew apart. Sceptics suggest this is just misperception, caused by the vagaries of human observation, I have certainly seen similar claims from UFO witnesses who were describing what was clearly a bolide or man-made space debris re-entry. Bearing this in mind, despite the conviction of those witnesses that the object changed course, it probably did not. Even so, according to calculations by W. Zabawski in 1977, who plotted the track of the fiery object from accounts by witnesses between Irkutsk and Vanavara, the object did seem to weave about before

23

detonating over the swamp.

However, perhaps the most significant findings are the shiny balls embedded into tree stumps within the impact zone. These are not unlike tektites, found in some meteorite craters. Tektites are created by the intense heat fusing sand and rock into glassy fragments. Not surprisingly, they have also been discovered at the sites of nuclear detonations, where huge amounts of energy are produced. Thus the discovery of tektites in Tunguska means that the nuclear explosion theory cannot be dismissed out of hand.

Recently, some evidence has been found which may rule out a comet once and for all. The evidence concerns the speed at which the object was travelling when it exploded above the forest. Normally, this is calculated by reference to the amount of kinetic energy that must be necessary to cause the observed devastation. At Tunguska this matches an extremely fast-moving object – moving at a speed similar to a comet impacting with the earth's atmosphere.

However, there are several problems. For instance, it is now known that there were two shock waves: one caused by the explosion and a slightly earlier one resulting from the air displacement as the object (be it comet or spaceship) passed above the forest. The air-displacement shock wave only indicates a speed of at most a few thousand mph: far too slow for a comet. In addition, the eyewitnesses all spoke of seeing and hearing the object pass over simultaneously. Yet, if the object were travelling at many times the speed of sound, then, just as with a thunderstorm, where the sound (the thunder) lags behind the vision of the electrical discharge (the lightning), there should have been a similar delay reported. There was not.

Furthermore, if the object exploded at just 5 km (3 miles) above the ground, as the evidence suggests, and it was moving at, perhaps 40,000 km/hr (25,000 mph), then it should have been visible for much less time than eyewitness reports indicate – and moving at a far greater apparent speed. Their testimonies either imply an object that was much higher in the atmosphere (i.e., further away from the ground observers) – which is not what the detonation evidence indicates – or else something that was moving a good deal more slowly than a comet normally does. The difficulty is that, if this were true, and the object had a far smaller velocity than scientists are assuming, its kinetic energy would be too low to produce the explosive destruction and thermal effects all too evident from the site. Only one thing could explain that discrepancy: if the relatively slow-moving, low-flying object blew apart as a result of a nuclear, rather than a conventional, explosion.

The debate rages on.

1925:
A METEOR OVER MONTANA

This case rests solely on the account of John Cross from Polson, Montana, a remote ranching area in the north-west of the USA. The incident occurred in late September or early October 1925, just after dusk. Aside from John, then a young child, his mother was also witness to what happened.

John told me how a 'pulsating, roaring noise' made them look upwards to see 'a flaming circular object of approximately 60 m (200 ft) or more in diameter descending at approximately 1,100 to 1,600 km/hr (700 to 1,000 mph) and about 8 km (5 miles) distant.'

Obviously, these are subjective judgements compromised by the passage of over 60 years before Cross reported the matter to me. However, he adds that the device was clearly rotating 'at the rate of about two turns per second'. From the noise it made, he felt that it had been damaged and was crashing out of control. Cross estimates that it was in view for about 5 seconds and fell at a 45-degree angle, seeming to crash behind a distant mountain west of his family's ranch. A brilliant flash of white light lit the sky at the point where it appeared to strike the earth, but no sound or shock wave followed.

I immediately thought that this was a story about a bolide or fireball meteor. That one should impact in Montana in 1925 is not impossible, even though I can trace no record of one having done so. Most members of the general public in an age without TV and widespread interest in space would not have known what a bolide was, or recognize what one looked like if they chanced to see one fall. Indeed, today, many people are unfamiliar with them. In February 1994, when we appeared on a chat show together in Belfast, I was able to explain to TV presenter David Jacobs that an object he had seen in October 1983, in the company of ex-UK politician Shirley Williams, was, almost certainly, a bolide. He was not familiar with their

25

existence and seemed pleased that there was an explanation for the mysterious flying object. If these phenomena are a mystery to knowledgeable and intelligent people now, then that is all the more reason to assume that they could have baffled someone far off the beaten track in 1925.

However, there are some problems with the bolide theory. The sound effects, while not unknown, are unusual. Similarly, the rotation is something not recognized in other cases of this kind. Furthermore, John Cross says categorically that there was no fiery trail in the object's wake, as one might expect, but that he did see pieces of debris being thrown off and disintegrating as they fell from the main body towards the ground.

Another problem is the object's speed. Cross insists that he heard the object before he saw it. This is just not possible, if it was kilometres high in the atmosphere and travelling at the high speed of a fireball meteor. Cross himself felt it was moving very low above the surface at possibly sub-sonic speed, but he was puzzled by the lack of sound of an impact explosion. That might suggest that it did not hit ground at all, or, if it did, that this was further than the 8 km (5 miles) away that he estimates. Cross added something else of interest: he said that midway through the flight, the object 'seemed to hesitate and move approximately one diameter to the north before it continued its descent'. Ranch hands immediately went out to check on the cattle and horses and found them very restless and close to the point of stampeding.

Nobody visited the remote mountain area in the wake of this experience until about 25 years later, in 1950, when John and his father went there to do some logging. They discovered a large burnt area of ground, which might have suggested something ablaze had struck the earth. But they did not connect the two events until much later, by which time it was long forgotten.

1946:
NAZI SPACESHIPS INVADE SCANDINAVIA

Throughout the latter stages of World War 2, pilots of the Allied forces saw strange objects in the sky. They appeared mostly over Europe and were given the nickname 'Foo Fighters'. At first it was assumed that these were secret weapons developed by the Nazis. They resembled glowing lights that dogged aircraft but never attacked them.

UK comedian Michael Bentine, then an intelligence officer supervising the free Polish forces, told me of the debriefings he carried out in late 1944 on aircrew who had seen the lights during raids on the secret V-rocket base at Peenemunde and the intense interest in them shown by US intelligence staff. Despite feeling they were dangerous, no crewman ever described a single harmful effect caused by them.

American researcher Barry Greenwood has uncovered many records from war-time personnel describing the Foo Fighter encounters between autumn 1944 and spring 1945. There were dozens of sightings. Nobody ever seems to have resolved what they were and no evidence captured from the Third Reich after the fall of Berlin indicates that Germany was behind the incidents. However, in 1980 W.A. Harbinson wrote an epic novel entitled *Genesis*. Although it is fiction, he includes a detailed factual afterword to indicate that he based it on documentary research. I understand that his research continues and that Harbinson intends eventually to publish a much expanded version of his work. Essentially, Harbinson contends that papers he has uncovered discuss how the Nazis built small, remote-controlled, circular craft whose engines ionized the atmosphere, causing it to glow. They were sent up against aircraft partly to cause panic and partly as an anti-radar deterrent.

According to Harbinson, this was only the beginning of the story. In keeping with plans to extend the V-2 rocket into an intercontinental V-3 (capable of bombing New York and seemingly close to operational use as the war ended), the Germans were also working furiously on the Foo Fighter (or *Feuerball*, as they had termed it) to produce a piloted version, code-named the *Kugelblitz*. Harbinson also claims that an aeronautical pioneer, Rudolph Schriever, had built a prototype Foo Fighter in 1942 and was preparing to put it into production when the war ended. With the fall of Germany imminent, the prototype and plans were destroyed to prevent it from falling into enemy hands. Other reports state that the fighter was not successfully test flown from a base in the Harz Mountains until 14 February 1945. Intriguingly, Greenwood's independent search of Foo Fighter records, many years after Harbinson's book appeared, found that all cases from February 1945 focused closely around that specific date.

Harbinson's claims enter more contentious territory when he speculates about the Antarctic bases where the Foo Fighter was developed further by renegade Nazis who escaped the fall of Germany and whose research was to become the source of subsequent UFO encounters.

What is more interesting is that within a year of the alleged Harz Mountain test flight, strange things were reported flying over Scandinavia in alarming numbers. The reports began early in 1946 and spread from Finland to Sweden, where most sightings eventually concentrated. Over 1,000 reports were documented by the end of the summer of 1946, when the sightings dwindled and then stopped altogether. But that was not before there had been official panic, with a Swedish government inquiry, visiting high-level people from the UK and the USA evidently sifting through the data and – when fears about invasion intensified – what amounted to a temporary Press blackout of the news.

Extensive research into what has been called the 'ghost rocket' affair has been carried out by Anders Liljegren and Clas Svahn in Scandinavia. They have unearthed documents and pieced together a detailed picture of what took place. What is clear is that many of these projectile-like masses moving at great speed across the sky were simply misperceptions of meteors. After all, thousands of people were being alerted to watch the skies, primed by the reports, so many saw such natural phenomena for the first time. However, some sightings were not so easily explained – a conclusion reached by the Swedish government inquiry.

The Swedes were, of course, concerned – as were the visiting British and American defence people – that the overflights might be the USSR using Nazi hardware captured from secret bases on the eastern side of the Iron Curtain. The allies knew (as shown in secret documents from this time) that the Germans were extremely advanced in aircraft and weapons development at the end of the war. Most of the projects were in their early stages, but had the war continued into 1946, then things might have been very different. Knowing this, and never having solved the Foo Fighter mystery from the year before, there was a fear that the Soviets had got hold of – and were perfecting – technology which would give them a terrible advantage.

But why fly these things over Sweden, given the remote areas of the USSR that could be employed? Also, as is obvious in retrospect, if the Russians had such devices in 1946, why were they so far behind the Americans in the development of rocket and ballistic missile technology? It made no sense, and that was the real concern. What if these objects were not from the USSR, but came from somewhere else much further afield? A document dated 9 September 1946 reveals the British Air Ministry's secret discussion of the problem. It described the phenomenon as comprising wingless, torpedo-shaped craft that had a white core which was surrounded by a bluish-green glare. The craft were about the size of the full moon in appearance and usually silent. By 10 October, official statements referred to 'clear, unambiguous observations' which 'cannot be explained as natural phenomena' and how 'echo, radar and other equipment registered readings but gave no clue as to the nature of the objects'.

However, what interests us is that there were reports of crashes by ghost rockets. Most of these were either misperceptions (i.e., an optical illusion caused by the arcing flight of the object) or unproven. In one case, from near Björkon, Sweden, on 10 July 1946, slaglike material was extracted from a beach at a point where an impact was alleged by witnesses. Some of this was sent to England for analysis by defence specialists, who found that it was merely coke or some similar substance that had probably been on the beach long before the ghost rockets flew. This solution was put forward for all other ghost rocket crashes.

Intriguingly, in one case there was intense secrecy about the recovery of debris and it was this case that Liljegren and Svahn found most mysterious. The incident occurred on 19 July 1946, at about noon, in the vicinity of Lake Kolmjarv, Sweden. Witnesses on the shore reported seeing one of the ghost rockets plunge into the lake and disappear from view beneath a plume of water. The military were immediately alerted and spent three weeks searching the area. Officially, they failed to discover anything in the deep mud at the bottom of the lake, but this seems inconsistent with the amount of effort put into the investigation. It also seems out of phase with research by the latter-day Swedish UFO experts. In 1984 Liljegren and Svahn tracked down and interviewed surviving eyewitnesses and military investigators of the Lake Kolmjarv crash. They found complete mystification was still evident.

Karl Gosta Bartoll had led the search. He told Svahn that their investigation suggested that the object largely disintegrated in flight. He pointed out that one witness saw a second spray of water after the main fall, which supported this opinion. He added that the military concluded the object was 'probably manufactured in a light-weight material, possibly a kind of magnesium alloy'. Bartoll insisted that 'what people saw were real, physical objects'.

CHAPTER TWO

THE SUMMER THAT CHANGED THE WORLD

On 24 June 1947 a private pilot, called Kenneth Arnold, spotted some strange aircraft as he flew over the Cascade Mountains in Washington state, USA. An enterprising journalist picked up on his description that they moved 'like saucers skipping across water' and named the objects 'flying saucers'. A new phrase was born and with it a remarkably persistent craze.

In fact, Arnold's sighting was not the first, or the most interesting, of a wave of UFO events that had begun the month before. His sighting was merely the one that gained the most public attention and led to every American searching the skies for a glimpse of these strange visitors. For two weeks after Arnold's 'flying saucer' first hit the news wires, local and national papers (occasionally international ones, too) treated it as a major story. Every new saucer sighting was eagerly reported. Inevitably, there were jokers. In early July, in Louisiana, an object made from a metal dish (possibly a trash-can lid) was found smoking in the street. For a time it was thought to be of great importance and the army was called in to remove it. Painted on to it were the words 'Made in the USA' – and the nature of the crude hoax thus became apparent. However, this little jape was to have a more profound effect a few days later, when it came to be discussed by top men at the FBI.

In mid-July the US Army and Air Force asked the FBI to help to investigate the rising number of UFO reports which were beginning to swamp the military. A debate ensued internally within the FBI about whether to agree to this request. Its famed director, J. Edgar Hoover, noted on a memo that he, personally, would agree, but if the FBI helped, then the military would have to let it have access to all recovered discs. Hoover mentioned that in the 'La' case they had 'grabbed it' and the FBI had never seen it.

The FBI/US Army–Air Force co-operation lasted only a few weeks after it was initiated. A memo from its military partners was unwisely circulated around FBI offices, saying in effect that the US Army intended the FBI to deal with time-wasters, like 'discarded toilet seats and trash-can covers', thus leaving the military free to take on more important cases. Unsurprisingly, the FBI decided it had better things to do.

The 'La' saucer referred to by Hoover in the earlier memo was misinterpreted years later. The memo was made public in 1977 under the Freedom of Information (FoI) Act. As it dated from just a few days after the extraordinary events at Roswell, New Mexico, many have tried to connect the two, citing the memo as proof that a real saucer was recovered by the military, regardless of their protestations to the contrary. Hoover's handwriting could allow 'La' to be read as 'Sw'. Since Roswell is in the south-west of the USA you can – just about – stretch the facts to make it fit. Sadly, the truth is that Hoover clearly mentioned the recovered hoax disc affair and wrote 'La' on the memo – 'La' being the accepted abbreviation for the state of Louisiana.

Yet, despite this little piece of misleading evidence, something truly remarkable does appear to have occurred in the New Mexico desert just before the head of the FBI had penned these confusing words. It was to be a case that would make UFO history and, even half a century later, it is still thought by many people to be the most significant incident that has ever occurred. Let's see if it deserves such a description.

1947:
THE DAY THEY CAUGHT A SAUCER

The year 1955 saw the very first issue of *Flying Saucer Review*, a UK magazine destined to become influential over the next two decades. Inside it there was a remarkable story, although, at first, it seemed like merely another anecdote, nothing special. At the time, few saw the story's significance and it was to be many years before this was recognized by researchers. In fact the witness, Hughie Green, was later to become a popular figure in UK television.

In 1947 Green was serving with the Royal Canadian Air Force (although erroneously reported as an RAF man by *FSR*). In early July he made the long cross-country drive from California to Philadelphia, a journey which would take him through the inhospitable deserts of the south-western states. During this trip Green tuned into a radio programme which

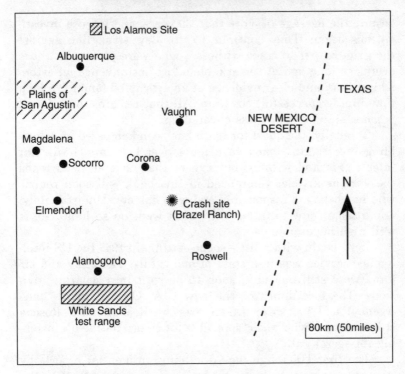

The site of the Roswell, New Mexico, crash in July 1947.

revealed how the US Army had been sent to investigate a flying saucer. It had apparently crashed in the New Mexico
desert. Further news flashes throughout that day added extra
details. Then there was silence. When he arrived in
Philadelphia, Green bought all the newspapers, but not one
featured anything about the saucer. It was never mentioned
again.

In fact, what Green had heard was the story released to
the local media in Roswell, New Mexico, on 8 July 1947. This
tale was debated by some early ufologists before being forgotten, because it was quickly discredited by the media. In any
event, yarns about crashing spaceships were considered
extremist nonsense by most of the first researchers. By the
time they were legitimized, early Press accounts had long been
erased from people's memories.

Not until early 1978 did anybody recall the Roswell story.
Then one of the airmen responsible for the news decided to tell
his version of events when he retired. The case was reopened,

despite the passage of more than 30 years, and intense investigations began. They continue to this day, struggling against the grim reaper to trace witnesses who were present at those events so long ago. A remarkable effort has unveiled an astonishing story and clear evidence of an attempted (and for a long time highly successful) cover-up. All that remains to be found is *what* kind of object was covered up.

Typically, the quest for truth has been hampered by squabbling investigator teams in dispute over key data. I will not infer rights and wrongs, but expect that anybody who reads the various articles referenced in this book will soon realize who has behaved responsibly and who has not. Unfortunately, any attempt now to fathom out what went on so long ago, is well nigh impossible.

Let's begin with a little scene-setting. In 1947 the US intelligence service was in a state of major flux. The army and air force were still one unit, soon to be split into separate divisions. The forerunner of the new CIA (Central Intelligence Agency) had just been taken over by Rear-Admiral Roscoe Hillenkoetter, who was responsible for co-ordinating all incoming top-secret data.

The first UFO sightings (including influential reports by military personnel) have to be seen in context with the response to the Foo Fighters two years earlier and the ghost rockets over Scandinavia a few months previously. Strange craft reportedly flying over the USA in the Cold War could not possibly be ignored. Within a few weeks, a major investigative unit had been set up to operate from Wright Patterson air force base in Dayton, Ohio. Officially, this unit (Project Sign) did not begin work until January 1948, but plenty of internal memos demonstrate that preliminary investigations began from early July 1947 onwards, including the abortive army–air force request for help from the FBI.

Curiously, however, from late July of that year investigating officers began to comment in now released memos about an anomaly. One USAF intelligence department report, dated 30 July, refers to the 'lack of topside inquiries' about UFOs compared with Foo Fighters and ghost rockets, and how this suggested that the flying discs might be a 'domestic project about which the President, etc., know.' This was not the only suspicion of the kind expressed during the first few years.

Of course, there is another possibility for that seeming lethargy. Earlier in July something dramatic may have happened which gave solid proof to high government people and made requests for news on current sightings less important than before. The capture of a crashed flying saucer would certainly fulfil that criterion, as all effort would then go into studying its physical make-up and probing this fortuitously procured hard evidence. The need for extensive data on vague lights spotted in the sky would be much reduced. That UFOs were simply not being treated with utter contempt by top military and government personnel is readily illustrated. In 1957 Rear-Admiral Hillenkoetter joined NICAP (National Investigation Committee into Aerial Phenomena), the first active national UFO group to proclaim a government cover-up.

In 1947 Roswell, New Mexico, was a small town famed for having the only air force unit in the world trained to drop nuclear weapons. The scrub landscape was surrounded in the west by facilities like White Sands Proving Ground, Alamogordo, where amazing new weapons and rocket systems were being developed and the first atom bomb had been detonated two years earlier. Roswell would continue to be of prime importance throughout the Cold War and remain a highly sensitive area.

The *Roswell Daily Record* for Tuesday, 8 July 1947 carried the front-page headline 'RAAF captures flying saucer on ranch in Roswell region'. This bold, detailed account echoed the data also going out onto the news wires and to the radio stations to be picked up by listeners like Hughie Green. The *Record* said how 'the intelligence office of the 509th bombardment group at Roswell Army Air Field (RAAF) announced at noon today that the field has come into possession of a flying saucer ... According to ... Major J.A. Marcel ... the disc was recovered on a ranch in the Roswell vicinity, after an unidentified rancher had notified Sheriff George Wilcox, here, that he had found the instrument on his premises.' Note the curious use of the word *instrument*, as opposed to craft, machine or ship. The paper explained that the base intelligence officer had inspected the 'instrument' and that it was being flown to 'higher headquarters'.

Under release by the FoI, we now have access to the original Press release written by Lieutenant Walter Haut, who was the Roswell PIO (public information officer). It was completed at about 11 am that Tuesday after a morning meeting between senior officers of the base where the discovery of the wreckage had been discussed. Haut hand-delivered it to both Roswell radio stations and also to the town's two newspapers. The memo began:

> The many rumours regarding the flying disc became a reality yesterday when the intelligence officer [at Roswell] ... was fortunate enough to gain possession of a disc through the co-operation of one of the local ranchers ... The flying object landed on a ranch near Roswell some time last week. Not having phone facilities, the rancher stored the disc until such time as he was able to contact the sheriff's office ... Action was immediately taken [by the RAAF] and the disc was picked up at the rancher's home. It was inspected at the RAAF and subsequently loaned ... to higher headquarters.

Haut has since confirmed that the Press release was issued on the orders of Roswell base commander, Colonel William Blanchard, apparently with approval from Washington.

However, within minutes of the news hitting the wires, the base officers, Haut, all Roswell media sources (and, one presumes, the Pentagon) were swamped with calls from reporters world-wide, but mostly from within the USA. It seems that everyone had underestimated the interest in this story.

Within three or four hours there were new orders from Washington and the situation had changed dramatically. A follow-up story was released to the Press around tea-time that day which completely defused all the furore. The change in tone can be seen in another FoI release, a memo timed at 6.17 pm that Tuesday; a teletype, marked 'Urgent', sent from the FBI office in Dallas, Texas, to its offices in Ohio. It explained how they had been 'telephonically advised' by a senior air force source (Major Curtan of the Eighth Air Force HQ) that 'an object purporting to be a flying disc was recovered near Roswell, New Mexico, this date'. (An error, as the original Press release states that the discovery was several days earlier.) The FBI report adds that

> The disc is hexagonal in shape and was suspended from a ballon by cable, which balloon was approximately 20 feet in diameter. Major Curtan advised that the object found resembles a high-altitude weather balloon with a radar reflector, but that telephonic conversation between this office and Wright Field [i.e., Wright Patterson air force base] had not borne out this belief. Disc and balloon being transported to Wright Field by special plane for examination. Information provided this office

because of national interest in case and fact that national broadcasting company, Associated Press, and others attempting to break story of location of disc today.

This appears to be an intermediary version of events between the original dramatic lunchtime news and the early evening Press conference held in Fort Worth to dismiss it all. The results of that conference made several newpapers the following day and these left readers in no doubt. The *Roswell Daily Record*, for instance, carried a new front-page story. 'General Ramey empties Roswell saucer', which described how an examination of the debris at Fort Worth, Texas, by the head of that base, 'revealed last night that the mysterious object found on lonely New Mexico ranch was a harmless high-altitude weather balloon – not a grounded flying disc'.

There are interesting clues in all of these Press releases. Firstly, the Haut memo is excited and affords little doubt that the Roswell base believed they had hold of a flying saucer. Yet the paper used 'instrument', a term far more in keeping with later weather balloon claims than a spaceship or extraordinary aircraft. We do not seem to know why this was. Then, as the story hit the wires and the wreckage was flown on to 'higher headquarters' a rapid change of tack followed the unexpected media barrage. Now, the Press were told that it was all a big mistake: the UFO was just bits of an old balloon. Yet, the FBI memo issued at the same time that evening (seemingly via a reputable air force source and possibly taking into acount the FBI's slightly enhanced 'need to know'), only noted that the thing 'resembles' a balloon but that this suggestion itself was allegedly 'not borne out' when the allegation was checked.

Naturally, the version that most rational people have tended to accept, and which seems all too plausible, is that the object really was a balloon. The second release simply corrected an error of over-exuberance from Roswell. Perhaps so, but this fails to explain why all the senior officers at a major air force base could not identify a weather balloon – surely, something familiar to most military personnel. Moreover, why take the unprecedented step of going public, in this big way, without forethought? Equally, who gave permission from higher up for them to do so?

Note also – perhaps crucially – that even at 6.17 pm, when publicly the 'it was just a balloon' story was being issued by General Ramey at Fort Worth, the FBI was told that debris was still being sent on from there to Wright Patterson. Indeed, the memo closes by saying that the FBI would next endeavour to learn the results of the official analysis to be done at Dayton. If this really had all been a mistake, and the debris was now positively identified as a mere balloon, then why was a special plane still sending this junk on to headquarters in Ohio? It seems contradictory.

You can see why the balloon story did its job and turned off both the media and UFO enthusiasts from any further investigation at the time. To unravel the many mysteries surrounding the affair, let's turn to first-hand testimony from those who were actually involved.

In 1978, Ohio investigator Leonard Stringfield was collating data on UFO crashes, or what he called 'retrievals of the third kind'. His work was first presented in a lecture to the UFO group MUFON that July and he has published a steady stream of 'Status Reports' ever since, which have been invaluable in forging research into several alleged incidents. Between February and April 1978, Stringfield was one of the three UFO investigators (the other two being William Moore and Canadian Stanton Friedman) who talked to a retired air force major, whom Stringfield called 'JM' in his first status report (published in 1979). From reference to FoI documents and research into 1947 Press stories, it was soon obvious to anyone who checked this out that JM was the actual intelligence officer named in the *Roswell Daily Record* who had first inspected the debris. He was Major Jesse Marcel, a man with an impeccable service record who, true to his allegiance to the air force, had remained silent about the events at Roswell until the FoI released some data about it. Moreover, in retirement, he felt more free to talk. Marcel gave many interviews, including some on tape and film, before hs death in 1986. He was, of course, a vital first-hand witness.

According to Marcel, a sheep rancher had discovered the wreckage some days before (apparently on Thursday, 3 July) and taken it into Roswell on his next visit (Sunday, 6 July). Despite the frequent reference to Roswell by most books, TV shows and movies in connection with the crash site, the rancher actually lived in Lincoln County near the town of Corona, some 130 km (80 miles) north-west of Roswell. It is no surprise that it took three days for this isolated ranch foreman to report the matter, or that he chose Roswell, which was bigger than Corona and had a major air base. However, instead of going first to Sheriff George Wilcox, as any responsible citizen

38

probably would have done, Wilcox went straight to Marcel, taking some small pieces of the UFO with him. Marcel was baffled by them, so returned to the ranch, accompanied by Captain Sheridan Cavitt, a counterintelligence specialist. This suggests that the Roswell base were concerned about the possible enemy source of the wreckage right from the start. It seems hard to imagine that both these senior officers had never seen a weather balloon; the rancher's pieces of metal were obviously unfamiliar to them, so they decided to investigate further. The rancher told the air force officers how the debris was scattered over a wide area (later measured as about 2.6 sq km/1 sq mile; again, patently an absurd area for something the size of a weather balloon).

The two Roswell officers reached the ranch late that Sunday evening and they stayed overnight at the foreman's homestead. In the meantime, Sheriff Wilcox says he had sent two deputies to the crash site. Without the rancher to guide them, they did not find any debris, but they did discover an area blackened by fire. On the Monday, the sheriff sent a couple of deputies, with more precise information, to the crash location, but they were turned away by an army road block before they got there.

On the Monday afternoon, back at Roswell, the bits of UFO debris were on a plane to the regional air force headquarters at Carswell in Fort Worth, Texas, where they arrived under the supervision of General Roger Ramey. By then, Marcel and Cavitt had nearly finished collecting all the wreckage they could find, and they were loading it into a truck to take back to Roswell. According to Marcel, the wreckage was extraordinary stuff: a lot of dull, greyish, foil-like material which was very thin yet incredibly durable. He described trying to bend or dent it, but it was resistant even to impact from a sledgehammer, despite being extremely light. (One of the pilots who flew the crated wreckage to Fort Worth was traced and told the investigators that the crate weighed very little for its size.) Aside from this foil, there was also a parchment-like material and something that resembled balsawood. There were thin beams with curious markings etched on them in purple or pink colours, which have been described as hieroglyphics. Note how some of the UFO crashes from the nineteenth century had curiously similar details.

Reaching Roswell around 2 am, Marcel stopped at his home to show the debris to his wife and son. Clearly, he believed he was holding something amazing. Radiation readings at the site had demonstrated that it was safe.

A meeting at the air force base followed later that same morning (8 July) and resulted in Haut's Press release. Then came the media attention that continued throughout the rest of Tuesday afternoon, being defused finally by the revelations at Fort Worth that evening which claimed that the object was just a weather balloon. Marcel was always very explicit about the debris he recovered. He told investigators that 'The material I gathered did not resemble anything off a balloon. A balloon of any kind could not have exploded and spread its debris over such a broad area.' He never shifted from his conclusion that what he saw in 1947 was the remains of an alien craft. He said that he was told by General Ramey at Fort Worth (where he took the remainder of the wreckage that Tuesday afternoon *en route* to its final destination at Wright Patterson in Ohio) that the story of a weather balloon was to be used as a cover to get the Press off their backs; they needed time to study the wreckage and find out what it was.

Of course, this cover story, if that is what it was (and the facts certainly appear to support this), only succeeded for one reason: the material described by Marcel sounds very curious for pieces of a spaceship that has travelled the universe. Yet, bits of thin wood, tin foil and parchment stained with hieroglyphics can easily be considered as parts of a twisted balloon without stretching credulity all that far. The main anomaly was their reputed durability. Had the debris been anything more substantial, or undoubtedly from a wrecked aerial craft, then such a cover story could never have worked. Of course, who can know what an alien craft would look like?

There have been critics – and not only debunkers – of Marcel's testimony. He has been quoted by ufologists as saying that photographs taken of him at Fort Worth alongside bits of debris actually depict the real alien wreckage. One of these appeared (heavily cropped) in some early sources. When it is seen in full frame, it illustrates beyond much doubt that Marcel is really standing in front of the battered remains of the weather balloon which General Ramey later put on display for reporters and a Press photographer. The photo was taken in several people's presence, including one of his first officers, Colonel Thomas DuBose, and base meteorologist Irving Newton, who was brought into Ramey's office to identify the balloon publicly. Marcel is also cited elsewhere saying that the photographs of him taken at Fort Worth do not show the real wreckage, only the balloon.

Benevolent sceptic, Chris Allan, also noted in *International UFO Reporter* in May 1993 that it seemed odd that, if Marcel thought the matter so important, he had kept no records of the case, not even Press cuttings. Others have responded that this shows the proper military bearing of the man, giving the imposed secrecy about the affair that he accepted. I have to say that most things I have seen or heard Marcel say about the case have been credible and I have no difficulty accepting his word. But luckily we are by no means dependent upon his testimony alone.

In 1991 in *MUFON UFO Journal*, researcher Paul Fischer described tracking down and speaking to Jesse Marcel Jr, the Roswell officer's son. Now a grown man, he easily recalled that incredible night when he was 11 and he was roused from sleep to see the wreckage which his father had brought back from the desert. Quashing rumours from some more excitable sources, and thus enhancing his own position, Dr Marcel told how his father had never professed to seeing alien bodies at the crash site. Dr Marcel particularly remembered one piece of wreckage – like a beam about 30 to 45 cm (12 to 18 in) long – which had symbols upon it that were embossed in some curious way and coloured violet or grey. He has been able to sketch these from memory and they are more akin to an unidentifiable symbolic language than hieroglyphics, although there is some resemblance.

In 1980 the early written material on Roswell was brought together by ufologist William Moore. As it was still very thin, it was fleshed out by best-selling author Charles Berlitz with what can fairly be described as some padding. A slim book, *The Roswell Incident*, was the result. Although it was really premature to debate the matter properly, it put the case on the map and served to stimulate other witnesses to come forward; as such it is unfair to be too critical about it. I did something similar with two colleagues in 1983 when compiling a book during very early phases of the investigation into the Rendlesham Forest incidents. It can be useful to try to coax people out of the shadows, although the danger is, of course, that at the same time you brief them about what you know concerning the case.

In July 1982 William Moore presented a progress report on the case to a MUFON convention in Toronto, Canada. He had found and spoken with a number of new witnesses, including Lieutenant Walter Haut, the man who issued the Press release, and Frank Joyce, a radio journalist in Roswell who was the first person to be given the information. Both confirmed the gist of the story and how a big fish from Washington kicked up a stink almost as soon as Joyce put the story on the wires. Haut was threatened with immediate transfer and told he had screwed up in a big way by making the story public. Based on his interviews with the rancher, Joyce also hinted that more complete wreckage, and possibly even alien bodies, may have been recovered from the desert.

The ranch foreman, William 'Mac' Brazel, had died long before any investigator could interview him. However, his children were able to fill out the details supplied by his neighbours, the media and air force sources. It seems that during a major storm on the night of 2 July a strange explosion (unlike thunder) was heard by Brazel. Next day, he rode out to check on the livestock and found the debris. There was, reputedly, a groove dug into the earth, which, if true, would be utterly inconsistent with the weather-balloon story.

After his first visit to Roswell, Brazel returned, at the invitation of the military, on the night when the 'weather balloon' story was being released from Fort Worth by Ramey. Brazel was then kept under virtual house arrest in Roswell for about a week. Again, this is ludicrous if the cover story were true. Those who saw him around town (usually accompanied by military officers) have said that he had a deadpan look about him and ignored them. Yet, on Wednesday 9 July, Brazel was taken to the local radio station and publicly supported the weather-balloon story. He now changed his account to say he had found the debris a month earlier (before the flying saucer craze had even started) and spoke of burnt rubber – one of the most notable features of the debris that had been on display in Ramey's office the day before. Everyone who was there mentions the stench in the room. Nonetheless, none of the Press releases or first stories reporting Brazel or Marcel's discovery of the debris describe this smell. Later, Brazel told his family that he had been asked to give this new interview by the air force, but he would not be drawn further. One of his neighbours also commented that after his 'house arrest' he was soon seen driving around in a new pick-up truck and that he and his wife bought a new house not long afterwards. However, suspicions that he was 'bought off' by the government have been repudiated by Brazel's surviving family. They all support the initial story and insist that something truly incredible fell on the ranch that day, but insist that their father's apparent wealth was probably just the result of Brazel's talent for saving his earnings.

Critical to much of what we should believe about the Roswell case is exactly what happened to the recovered debris after being flown to Carswell in Texas and then what transpired later in General Ramey's office on the evening of Tuesday, 8 July. This has been subject to intense evaluation. In 1988 a former air force intelligence officer and long-term ufologist, Kevin Randle, began a systematic reappraisal of the case in conjunction with the respected UFO group, CUFOS (Center for UFO Studies), founded in 1972 by the late Dr J. Allen Hynek. Donald Schmitt, one of CUFOS's special investigations officers, assisted Randle. Their partnership resulted in the book *UFO Crash at Roswell*, published in 1991, and its 1994 sequel, *The Truth About the UFO Crash at Roswell*. A 1994 TV movie was made in the USA, based upon the first of these books.

Randle and Schmitt's arrival on the case, in the wake of a decade of pioneering work by William Moore and Stanton Friedman, unsurprisingly resulted in some tension within ufology. However, I have been greatly impressed by their dedication; fresh eyes looking at a case as important as this one, can surely only enhance its credibility.

Much of Randle and Schmitt's early work on the case was published in *International UFO Reporter*, the CUFOS journal. Some of the articles were gathered into a self-published book from CUFOS, called *The Roswell Report*, which came out alongside the duo's mass-market paperback in 1991.

Among the useful things that Randle and Schmitt did was to scour the desert on the former Brazel ranch, seeking minute fragments that might have been left behind after the crash. Arriving more than 40 years after the incident, little was expected and nothing, in fact, was found. But it was worth the effort and investigations resulted in some new second-hand source witnesses coming forward.

Randle and Schmitt built up a picture of what had occurred in General Ramey's office after he had received the first samples of debris on either 6 or 7 July. It seems that even as Major Marcel was ordered to fly the rest of the material on to Wright Patterson in Ohio (stopping *en route* at Carswell),

Ramey had decided on the plan to use a battered balloon to put the media off from chasing the story any further. Marcel said as much; indeed, he noted that when he arrived he left some of the wreckage on Ramey's desk and was then invited to show the General the location of the crash site on a map. By the time the two officers returned, the real wreckage was gone and the balloon debris laid out on the floor. Marcel was asked to pose with this for some photographs (seemingly taken by a base officer) and then kept incommunicado until sent back to Roswell. He did not accompany the real wreckage on to Ohio, as intended. This was forwarded, even as Ramey was co-ordinating the release of the 'it was only a balloon' story to the Press. Presumably, news of Marcel's presence at Carswell may have provoked too many questions.

It seems that at around 4 pm that afternoon, J. Bond Johnson, a reporter with the *Fort Worth Star-Telegram*, was asked by his editor to go to Carswell with his camera. At the base he was taken to Ramey's office and shown the balloon wreckage. He took three (or possibly four) photographs of it in the presence of Ramey, Colonel Thomas DuBose and the meteorologist Major Irving Newton. These are the photographs that were flashed around the wires and they, too, are the ones most commonly seen in connection with the case.

As explained before, two or three photographs had been taken before Johnson's arrival which show Marcel with what appears to be the same debris. There is dispute as to whether he ever thought this was the real wreckage. Indeed, he claimed that Ramey did not reveal the weather balloon explanation until after the reporter left the base. But one of Johnson's photographs seems to show General Ramey standing by the wreckage of the balloon, holding the Press release that was issued to reveal this solution.

Whatever the truth behind this confusion, which was probably inevitable with any witness after the passage of so many years, we do know that Johnson went straight back to his newspaper and later met several waiting journalists, obviously primed to expect his report. They even had a portable wire machine with them so his photographs could be sent around the country for immediate release with the cover story. This had all been well set up in advance by someone – presumably at Carswell.

Johnson confirmed that the wreckage he was shown was made of very tough aluminium foil, balsawood, or things that

looked like them, and smelled of burnt rubber. His photographs back up his descriptions.

Eventually, Colonel Thomas DuBose was interviewed by
Randle and Schmitt. He was able to add very useful details.
According to him, Ramey ordered his men never to discuss the
matter ever again. DuBose added: 'We had orders from on high
to ship the material directly to Wright Field by special plane
... The weather balloon story was a complete fabrication
designed to get the reporters present off Ramey's back in a
hurry.' He noted further that he got a call from a senior officer in Washington that day who confirmed the cover-up. The
officer asked DuBose to ensure that the wreckage should be
packaged for his personal attention, and he ordered DuBose
not to discuss their phone conversation or the entire matter
either with General Ramey or even with his own wife!

Major Newton would only say that he was asked at the
last minute to confirm that some wreckage in Ramey's office
was a weather balloon – a conclusion Ramey had seemingly
already reached. Newton was in no doubt that what he was
then handed, and asked to be photographed standing alongside, was simply a balloon with parts of an attached hexagonal
radio device, commonly used to transmit data to the ground.

Thus, two of the three officers present in Ramey's office
that day (Marcel and DuBose) say that a balloon was substituted for the real wreckage (although whether Marcel thinks
real wreckage was ever photographed there remains more open
to doubt). Nothing that the meteorologist adds to the story
contradicts that view. The only missing source is Roger
Ramey, later promoted to brigadier-general and transferred to
a high-level job in the Pentagon. Even if he were still around
to be interviewed, it seems unlikely he would have risked
breaching top-level security to do so.

Taken all together, there is a very strong case to support
claims that the media was manipulated into believing that the
Roswell wreckage was unimportant and nothing but a weather balloon. Yet the testimony of all those who saw it on site,
or shortly afterwards, their apparent inability to identify it and
the way in which it was given priority shipment to the main
air force base in Ohio, all flatly contradict this.

Perhaps the balloon cover was invented to remove the
story from the media spotlight while official study of the
wreckage carried on in secret elsewhere. However, there are
some grounds to suspect that there might have been another

reason. Was attention deliberately being focused on Fort Worth, Texas, and General Ramey's office on Tuesday 8 July and the day after? Was this to distract any enquiries away from Roswell and the discovery of the crash site, because something even more extraordinary was going on here? Had the rest of the spaceship and its crew been found? There are some primary sources supporting this claim. The one most often cited comes from soil engineer Grady ('Barney') Barnett, who told family and friends in the early 1950s that he had seen a crashed UFO site. He died long ago and as a result we only have second- or third-hand versions to go by. Normally, that would be worthless. However, they deserve an airing if only because they are multiple and consistent and come from a time period when this case was not the subject of public knowledge; even so, they must be approached with caution.

According to family members, Barnett was out on the Plains of San Agustin, 160 km (100 miles) west of the Brazel ranch. The date was early July, around the same time when Brazel found the scattered wreckage. Barnett came upon a damaged but near-complete, disc-shaped craft embedded in the ground, with several bodies near by. They appeared dead. The creatures were child sized, had grey skins and pear-shaped heads and wore one-piece suits of silvery grey. A small party of archaeology students, led by a professor, were also in the area and saw this whole thing too, Barnett alleged. All of them, Barnett included, were then apprehended by a military unit that arrived to secure the site. They were reminded of their patriotic duty never to discuss the matter, which, seemingly, nobody ever did, apart from Barnett to a small degree.

A tall tale spun by someone widely said to have no history of deception? Perhaps. But, the presence of a second, nearby crash site with bodies would make the Roswell case more exciting. Moreover it would make some sense.

The few bits of debris on the Brazel ranch hardly constitute a spaceship. But what if the craft suffered an explosion as it flew over (which would explain the noise heard by the rancher), dropping bits of wreckage on to the ground; then the main body flew on until it impacted fatally in the Plains of San Agustin? The widespread debris described by Brazel and Marcel fits something that exploded in mid-air and perhaps spewed detritus as it flew westwards. It is hard to understand how a weather balloon of any description (or indeed any object that crashed from the sky) would not leave its remains over a far smaller area than the 1.6 sq km (1 sq mile) of devastation that was described north of Roswell.

Unfortunately, no evidence backs up Barnett. Checks with people in the San Agustin area have failed to trace memories of a crash – a contrast to the area around the Brazel ranch, where many locals seemed to know about it. If Barnett's story were unique, it would have little credence, but it is not: there are other claims about a second crash site. One was given to both William Moore and later to Randle and Schmitt by an air force officer called Lewis Rickett, who professed to have been part of the clean-up operation mounted by the Roswell base to bring in the wreckage. Unfortunately, his memory is a little hazy and it is unclear whether the events he describes occurred immediately after the crash or up to two months later. Nevertheless, Rickett says that he was responsible for liaising with Dr Lincoln La Paz, one of America's leading astronomers of the day and a world-renowned expert on meteorites. La Paz's forte was to plot eyewitness accounts and track these to the supposed impact point where a meteorite struck the ground, then locate debris for scientific evaluation. He also was conveniently local, based at the University of Albuquerque.

If there was any suspicion of a second impact point, then La Paz's involvement is readily understandable. He had top-secret security clearance and over the next five years often worked with the USAF on UFO-related projects. While documents about these matters have been retrieved under FoI release, nothing referring to his association with the Roswell case has ever emerged. However, the picture painted of La Paz by Edward Ruppelt, who was head of the USAF investigation into UFOs during the early 1950s, is interesting. In his 1955 memoirs, written after he left the air force, he describes meeting the scientist and discovering his undoubted interest in the subject. Dr J. Allen Hynek also often expressed his view that La Paz was fascinated by UFOs.

According to Rickett, he and La Paz spent weeks in the desert and recoverd some foil-like material and some glassy substance. La Paz reputedly told him he had found (but never showed him) a second site, some kilometres from the first crash spot. Here there was damage to tree tops and signs of an impact. The astronomer spoke about an unmanned 'probe' that he felt had landed, taken off again, exploded and then crashed.

However, Chris Allan again has doubts about this evidence. He points out that we know from released documents that between 1948 and 1951 La Paz worked with military authorities on a top-secret project, called 'Twinkle', whose aim was to trace mysterious green fireballs plaguing the area. They eventually staked out sites with expensive monitoring equipment, including one at Vaughn, only 48 km (30 miles) from the Brazel ranch. Apparently the green fireballs were worrying the authorities because of their proximity to sensitive nuclear and rocketry sites, such as Los Alamos. Indeed, a secret conference about them was held here in 1949 and attracted some of the most famous physicists in America, such as Dr Edward Teller, a leading mind behind the atomic bomb. Security clearances of all those present at Los Alamos, including La Paz, went through the roof.

Allan suggests that Ricketts is simply mixing up his dates, because we know that La Paz spent much time tracking eyewitness accounts and failing to find impact points for various 1948–49 green fireballs. Officially, the mystery of these lights was never solved and it remains a fascinating issue in the UFO world, especially given that almost identical green fireballs were reported 30 years later in the vicinity of that other well-known UFO crash site – Rendlesham Forest, in Suffolk, England.

Of course, if La Paz had been involved in the Roswell affair, then his later close association with the green fireball hunt is no surprise. Equally, the Roswell crash, if it happened as suggested, would have provided a real spur for the time, money and effort expended by top scientists into what, on the surface, seem to be fairly trivial sightings of green lights in the sky that occurred in the same part of New Mexico. Dr Lincoln La Paz was never interviewed about his possible involvement in the Roswell case, despite several attempts to do so before he died. His family insisted that he was too ill to speak over the phone whenever he was contacted on the matter. Although the Barnett and Rickett/La Paz stories are the main pointers to a second crash site, a host of other claims about the possible recovery of bodies have been found by Moore, Shandera, Stringfield, Friedman, Randle and Schmitt.

Captain Oliver ('Pappy') Henderson told his wife – and other people too, it seems – in 1981 about his involvement in the case. He did so after seeing publicity for the release of Moore's 1980 book and thus, he said, 'I guess I no longer have to keep it secret.' Henderson reported how he flew wreckage from Roswell to Dayton, Ohio, and confirmed that it was of a spaceship and that alien bodies were recovered with it. He implied that he saw these and described the bodies in a very similar manner to Grady Barnett.

Stringfield found another airman, 'Tim', who described flying a crate from Roswell to Fort Worth. He was never told what was inside, but the flight contained top-ranking officers and one of his crew spotted an air force mortician among them. Stories swarmed all over the base that alien bodies had been recovered along with the so-called weather balloon. Tim and his crewman commented that they were now a 'part of history'. Tim was later able to retrieve records which showed that his flight to and from Carswell was on 9 July. This fits perfectly, because he recalled flying Major Marcel back home to Roswell and Marcel had, as we have already seen, been kept at Carswell overnight and then returned on that very date, instead of flying on to Wright Patterson with the wreckage as anticipated.

Tim Good, a British researcher, was approached by the daughter of a GI who said that on his death-bed her father had spoken of a matter that he had also mentioned a few times before. He said that when he was stationed at Roswell air force base in 1947, he had helped in the recovery of three alien bodies from the desert.

Glen Dennis, a mortician in Roswell, described a curious call he got from the air base in July 1947. They were asking about the smallest size of coffins he had available. Dennis followed up by driving his hearse to the base, assuming there had been an air crash. He was practically thrown out, but he was later told by a nurse in the base hospital that there were three little bodies – two badly mangled, one more or less intact. She described how they had four fingers; the bone from the elbow to the wrist was longer than that from the elbow to the shoulder; how the whole body was surprisingly fragile and the eyes appeared oddly concave. These unusual details seem unlikely to have been just invented for effect.

This is all circumstantial and anecdotal evidence, but it does seem to be building towards a credible scenario. However, the outstanding question concerns the whereabouts of the archaeologist and his students who supposedly saw the bodies. If any of these people could be traced, then the second crash-site story would gain new impetus. Without them, Grady Barnett's tale – which, in effect, had launched all reference to aliens within this case (for Marcel and Brazel appear never to have talked about them) – would be very difficult to support. The search for the archaeologists has been a primary focus of UFO research during the first half of the 1990s. At the time of writing, no one has been found, although the hunt continues. Thomas Carey, an anthropologist as well as a CUFOS researcher, has reported on his extensive and painstaking effort to trace the team that might have been on the San Agustin Plains in July 1947. Indeed, so exhaustive has this been that his negative findings almost constitute elimination of the option that a UFO did crash in the San Agustin area that summer. He has yet to search for any expeditions that might have been nearer to Brazel's ranch.

Much controversy grew up around Gerry Anderson, a man who came forward in January 1990 after the hit TV show *Unsolved Mysteries* featured the Roswell case (including an illustration of Barnett's story). He alleged that, aged five, he was on the San Agustin Plains with his family and saw the second crash site and bodies, plus the archaeologists and Barnett. He even said the archaeology professor was called Dr Buskirk. It is worth noting that no version of Barnett's testimony from the 1950s referred to the presence on the site of a family with a young boy, in addition to the archaeologists whom he always spoke about.

In their recent book *Crash at Corona*, Stanton Friedman and Don Berliner present Anderson's story, suggesting that there were two crashes. However, Randle and Schmitt would not accept Anderson's story as it stood. Quite a debate erupted, which eventually moderated in February 1992 when both sides were brought together to thrash out their evidence privately at a well-organized symposium in Chicago, jointly operated by CUFOS and the Fund For UFO Research (which sponsors UFO projects). The transcripts of the papers, the debates and facsimiles of the evidence were published as *The Plains of San Agustin Controversy*, later that year. This is the best way of deciding for yourself who makes the strongest case about this new witness to the Roswell affair.

The book reveals that Anderson easily passed a lie-detector test and provided a few unpublished details seemingly supported by other Roswell witnesses. An archaeology professor called Dr Winfred Buskirk was traced, but demonstrated that he was not in the Plains area in July 1947, even though he did match Anderson's description and to most people's satisfaction was accepted as the same man. It was then established, by detective work, that in 1957 this professor was teaching at the college attended by the teenage Anderson, although Anderson insisted that he never met Buskirk.

So what really did happen in New Mexico in 1947? Is there any hope that we will ever find out? Surprisingly, the answer is yes. We may be close. It seems quite clear that the weather balloon claim was meant to act as a smokescreen to rebuff the Press. This means that something much more sensitive had to be involved, but by itself this far from proves that the UFO hypothesis is correct, of course. Other options have been contemplated, some of which we will now review.

Ufologist Ron Schaffner presented a credible scenario based upon his study of rocketry experiments on the White Sands Proving Grounds west of Roswell. Captured Nazi V-2s were used in a systematic series of tests (some secret, others not) from 1945 onwards. That year one veered off course and was heading for the town of San Antonio when it was detonated. Another crashed on a graveyard just across the Mexican border on 29 May 1947, only five weeks before the Roswell incident. Launches were temporarily suspended after that disaster, in which by pure good luck nobody was injured.

In the same week as the Roswell affair, a new V-2 test occurred, but, according to Press reports, the rocket blew up on take-off, injuring some technicians in the process. All of this makes the possibility of a stray V-2 crashing into Brazel's ranch far from absurd. Even the bodies have a potential explanation because monkeys were used as 'pilots' in some early V-2 tests, although these did not reputedly begin until 1948. Schaffner speculated that a rogue V-2, maybe containing some monkeys, crashed and was inevitably subjected to a major cover-up by the military. Had the truth emerged so soon after the Mexico incident, V-2 testing might have gone on to long-term hold for being far too dangerous.

The researchers into the Roswell case note these things, but they are unconvinced by them, pointing out that other accidents were not hidden (either before or after July 1947) but, more importantly, that the Roswell debris does not resemble a small V-2, even if it had exploded in mid-flight.

Ufologist John Keel had another suggestion to offer for the culprit. On the surface, his idea seems ludicrous, but it has a lot going for it. He argues that the crashed object was a balloon that had been launched from Japan as a terror weapon against the USA! In fact, these so-called balloon bombs were launched in great numbers during late 1944 and early 1945 and about 1,000 of them made the treacherous high-altitude flight across the Pacific and impacted on American soil. Their high-explosive cargo did detonate on several occasions in the western states and a major cover-up was put into force. The reason is simple: the Americans did not want the Japanese to know that their secret weapon was actually working, lest flights became more frequent. However, this secrecy was abandoned in the late spring of 1945, when six picnickers came upon a balloon in Oregon and were killed when they handled what they had not been warned was a huge bomb. These were the only civilian deaths on the US mainland caused by enemy action throughout the entire war.

After this tragedy, the public were alerted to balloon bombs; inside three months, the war was over in any event, and all secrecy lifted. Major stories about the Japanese successes were published in prestigious sources, such as the *New York Times* and *Washington Post,* early in 1946. Balloon bombs continued to be found years after the war ended, just as in Britain the occasional live German bomb is still dug up from time to time during building or excavation work, even half a century after hostilities. Since the last known balloon bomb launch was in April 1945, Keel proposed that one had somehow circled the earth in the upper atmosphere for two years and then crashed on Brazel's land. This seems more far-fetched than an alien spacecraft for most believers and sceptics alike. Later, Keel modified the theory with the suggestion that a renegade Japanese commander, refusing to accept his nation's defeat, might have launched an attack as a gesture of defiance during the summer of 1947. Perhaps we might further speculate that his weapon was struck by lightning during the storm, exploded high above the earth and scattered its pieces over a wide area of Brazel's land. In fact, we might even propose a scenario where the balloon had been trapped in a crevice for the two years since the end of the war, was freed by the severe storm winds on 2 July and then detonated by a lightning strike when airborne.

This certainly has an air of credibility to it and dispenses with the need for a renegade military attack during peace-time. This theory fits to some extent, because both Marcel and Brazel described parchment, balsawood and dull foil. The balloon bombs were made of thick rice paper, wood and other materials not too far removed from the descriptions offered; even the stained writing in picture language is not impossible to perceive as Japanese. The detonation of the payload would explain the strange explosion heard by Brazel during the storm and why there was so much debris thrown about on the ground.

Indeed, the Japanese balloon bomb theory was actually first proposed by Brazel himself to one of his neighbours, after his return from 'house arrest' in Roswell. This is according to a throwaway line in Randle and Schmitt's book (page 43) that might be very important. Brazel seems to have implied that he learnt the identity of the object from the military during his incarceration. Of course, this idea is not without problems. The durability, alleged imperviousness to fire and other extraordinary features of the wreckage, would be absurd (and clearly render the claims and all reference to alien bodies untrue) if the case were the result of a balloon bomb. The secrecy is easier to handle, especially if there was some thought that a rogue Japanese attack was being mounted in 1947. The diplomatic repercussions of that are obvious and top security would inevitably follow. In fact, almost everything that resulted in the following days within the military channels is predictable if the object was a Japanese bomb.

However, what is clearly not so easy to square is Jesse Marcel's reaction: that he would not have identified it as a balloon bomb or discovered this fact soon enough is virtually impossible to believe. In which case why would he be so adamant 30 years later that it was something alien and no type of balloon? Indeed, the bottom line really is: why the secrecy now? The entire Roswell mystery could be blown out of the water by a matter-of-fact announcement that the object was a balloon bomb, subjected to understandable security at the time and obscured with a cover story as a weather device. Half a century later, nothing would be compromised by saying exactly that, and much abuse directed at the government's expense would be spared. The fact that silence still prevails – or rather that the absurd weather balloon theory is adhered to – is the most serious argument that something extraordinary – secret *even now* – was involved in the Roswell crash.

Exactly the same argument scuppers claims that the object was an experimental aircraft. However amazing such a device might have been in 1947, there could be no possibility that it would remain secret all these years later. It would be the simplest thing in the world to destroy all interest in this case by presenting records that show this object was the then top secret XYZ 123 project which would now, of course, be vastly inferior to virtually everything that took to the air. As such, it would hardly be in need of any security restriction this far down the track. No – whatever happened at Roswell clearly still has massive security implications and there seem precious few things that one can think of, other than the real crash of an alien spaceship, that might begin to qualify for that sort of extensive and longstanding classification.

In 1994 three dramatic new developments occurred in this remarkable case that simply refuses to die. Firstly, Randle and Schmitt launched their second book with a Press conference in Roswell. The book turns the story on its head, alleging that new witnesses, who contacted the authors after the first book (and new stories from old witnesses which at times vary from their first accounts), maintained that the UFO crashed much nearer to Roswell than previously believed. Moreover, this happened two or three days later than first assumed. The alien bodies also have a more prominent role to play in the new scenario, which in places overturns much of what was said earlier. The idea that one of the aliens survived the crash is even alleged by some sources! Frankly, I worry that what is a credible story is in danger of being sunk by an over-abundance of witnesses and testimony. There can be little doubt that some jokers will have entered the fray once the case received big publicity. It is certainly difficult to know these days who is being sincere, who is finding it hard to recall things accurately from so long ago and who, to be blunt, is riding the bandwagon of publicity stirred up by all the attention given to the case since 1991. I hope this does not hinder the investigation rather than bolster it.

In the summer of 1994 the TV movie *Roswell* was also released, with plans to give it a cinema airing in Europe. The film is based on Randle and Schmitt's first book, both of whom appear as extras! According to its executive producer, Paul Davis, writing in March 1994, they built the movie around Jesse Marcel, portraying him as a kind of crusading investigator for the truth after attending a Roswell reunion in 1977 and discovering the secrecy that surrounded the long-forgotten story. Quite what this movie, and Steven Spielberg's alleged interest in a Roswell project to tie in with its fiftieth anniversary in July 1997, will do to the calibre of the still accumulating evidence, remains to be seen. However, without doubt, the most important event of 1994 was the announcement in January that the GAO (General Accounting Office) has agreed to a request from US congressman Steven Schiff – himself urged on by various ufologists – to investigate the matter.

The GAO has a lot of teeth, having, for instance, top-secret clearances to access government files. It exists primarily to review whether proper government procedures were followed in contentious incidents, usually with a reference to financial expenditure. It has shown itself to be willing to publish damning evidence that might cause the White House problems – for example, exposing a scandal where residents of a town were exposed to high radiation doses during a secret experiment that was long hushed up.

Mark Rodeghier of CUFOS spoke with its staff and reported in March 1994 that the GAO does not consider that it is trying to find out what happened at Roswell and will interview no eyewitnesses. What it has agreed to do is use its independent status, and security clearances, to try to find any documentation about the matter that has been denied to the public. It is stressed by Rodeghier that this is not a bunch of UFO believers trying to prove their case. This is, as far as it is possible to tell, a wholly independent investigation with no vested interest in proving one thing or another. As such, it makes the GAO study perhaps the single most important outside investigation into the UFO subject that has ever happened.

In September 1994 part of the results of the GAO study were released. They proved a major disappointment for the ufologists. The US air force claim that the GAO traced records that show the UFO *was* a balloon, although not an ordinary one. It was part of Project Mogul, a secret experiment to float detection equipment high in the atmosphere and sense any nuclear detonations on Soviet soil. In 1947 there was an urgent need to find out how advanced Russian nuclear scientists had become – hence the cover-up. The fact that this simple truth was not revealed long ago may be suggested by the GAO to be a result of documentation being lost in a bureaucratic maze of departments. Of course, while the sceptics hail this news as vindication – it was just a balloon after all – the UFO believers feel there are many unanswered questions and are far from convinced it is game, set and match. The debate is sure to rage ever onward. Indeed, the full GAO enquiry, which will include analysis of FBI, CIA and other intelligence files, is not due to be released until late 1995.

CHAPTER THREE

TALL TALES
AND PHOTOGRAPHS

Things went very quiet in the immediate aftermath of the
Roswell affair. The episode was forgotten completely outside
the town itself by the time a retired marine, Donald Keyhoe,
appeared on the scene. After leaving the service and acting as
an aide to Charles Lindbergh, Keyhoe had begun a successful
writing career with a book about the pioneer aviator. Now, in
January 1950 he was set to publish the world's first UFO book.
Based on classic cases from the first two years (but excluding
the discredited Roswell affair, of course) and gradually building
towards the view that there was a government cover-up of
anything but wreckage and bodies, Keyhoe's clarion call
The Flying Saucers are Real sold half a million copies.
It rapidly became the talk of the world.
Almost single-handedly, Keyhoe's efforts created UFO research
and a plethora of local groups, followed by national associations
which continue to this day. His book was also to be emulated by
hundreds of further UFO titles which, by 1994, were appearing
more frequently than ever. With the floodgates opened by
Keyhoe, something very strange was about to be reported which
would cause major ripples among the American security forces.
At the time nobody quite understood why that was so; on the
face of it, the proffered story seemed absurd. Of course, if these
authorities knew something that most ordinary people did not –
namely the reality behind the events in Brazel's field in 1947 –
then what looks like over-reaction in response to a rather tall
tale may become somewhat more understandable. Perhaps they
thought the Roswell cover was about to be blown.

1948
THREE SAUCERS FALL TO EARTH

On 8 March 1950, within weeks of Keyhoe's book's publication,
there was a peculiar, almost unannounced lecture at the

University of Denver in Colorado. It was held, reputedly, during the lunch hour. In addition it was deliberately titled in a mysterious fashion as being just about 'science'; as such, it attracted a limited, mostly student, audience. But it was to have repercussions that spread far and wide.

Two months later (books were published remarkably rapidly in those days), Frank Scully, a freelance journalist for publications like *Variety*, produced his first and last book, *Behind the Flying Saucers*. It was, in effect, a detailed retelling of the Denver University lecture and the story reported there, with plenty of flowery language but no indication of any serious attempt to verify what had been claimed. According to Scully, the understated lecturer remained anonymous, but in the book he revealed that the man was a wealthy local businessman and former Yale student called Silas Newton, who worked in the oil industry. Newton reported in his lecture that in the late 1940s three flying saucers had crashed on North America and small alien beings had been found dead within them. All the saucers had come down in the Arizona/New Mexico region. Newton then described the aliens as being between 91 and 107 cm (3 to 3 ft 6 in) tall. They had no body hair, except for a slight downy fuzz like the skin of a peach. Two of the entities had allegedly survived the initial crash but subsequently died. As for the operation of the UFOs themselves, Newton claimed they used some kind of magnetic propulsion.

It is safe to say that few people took this story seriously. It had some local media attention and Scully's book sold well, but it did not set the world on fire. As no verifiable facts were offered, beyond some details of an alleged crash near Aztec, New Mexico in 1948, few ufologists got excited about the information. However, the book did ensure that the Roswell case was not reopened when all the witnesses were available to be interviewed, because most people thought Scully's book to be so outrageous that any other rumours about a crashed spaceship would be guaranteed short shrift.

According to Scully's report on the lecture – which he knew about because he was a friend of Newton's – one crash occurred in April 1948 about 20 km (12 miles) outside the town of Aztec, about 320 km (200 miles) south-west of Denver and a similar distance north-west of the Roswell crash site. In other words, it was again within a zone of sensitive military weapon testing that would prompt any local incident to be covered up, whatever its nature. Newton had been told of the crash, he claimed, by a professor who researched magnetic anomalies for secret government projects at places like Los Alamos. The professor, whom Scully merrily described as 'having more degrees than a thermometer', was given the pseudonym, 'Dr Gee'. Reputedly Dr Gee had been flown in by the air force to inspect the wreckage and he had analysed some of the propulsion systems of the craft after its retrieval. Newton had befriended Dr Gee, but he also later claimed that Gee was a composite character based on several researchers who had studied the crashed UFO.

Some further details offered by Scully are interesting. For example, he alleged that the UFO was made of a very light metal, like aluminium, which was very tough. Inside the craft some writing was found that had pictorial images, resembling Egyptian hieroglyphics. These two features do, of course, sound remarkably reminiscent of what we know about the Roswell case, but remember that not even the most dedicated UFO buffs had any knowledge of that affair in early 1950, although Newton could – just conceivably – have read some reports in the New Mexico Press three years earlier and incorporated a few details from them.

In September 1952 Scully's book was effectively blown out of the water by an exposé in *True* magazine, written by J.P. Cahn. *True* had carried positive UFO articles (for example, Keyhoe's first book was based on reports he had originally published there), so it was not an outright debunking publication. However, Cahn's investigation into Newton and the man he claimed was the real Dr Gee were devastating to the authenticity of the case. Newton was presented as a rather shady oil dealer and Dr Gee as one Leo GeBauer, who ran a shop supplying TV and radio components. Cahn said this was all a scam, possibly to try to whip up interest in oil-rich land around Aztec; the topical element of a 'flying saucer' was added for effect.

Frankly, most people saw this exposé as credible and the Newton–Scully claims appeared well and truly discredited. Scully never recovered and even today his book is widely viewed as a naïve presentation of a story he may well have believed, but which was clearly false. There are only a few who regard the matter in any other light, primarily because, unlike Roswell, witnesses were not coming forward to support the Aztec incident with interlocking stories. Even Randle and Schmitt, in their 1991 book about Roswell, say, unhesitatingly, that 'The only conclusion possible is that this case ... is a hoax.' However, they also note that some people have speculated that the government might have helped spin such a yarn to ensure the Roswell case was not reopened when UFOs became big news after Keyhoe's book; but giving ufologists another crash story would be a particularly risky form of diversionary tactic. It would probably have been sheer good fortune if it had worked and nobody rediscovered Roswell in the months following the publication of the Scully book, since some people must have been intrigued by his claims; had they scoured old newspapers for evidence, who knows what they might have unearthed.

Dr Robert Spencer Carr was one of the few people not put off by the Cahn exposé of this case. He was an expert in non-verbal communications at the University of South Florida. He spent years collating material and attempting to verify the Aztec crash, partly because he had lived in New Mexico at the time of its occurrence. Carr reported in March 1978 to Len Stringfield, then compiling his status reports. He claimed that three radar sites – in Colorado, in California (Edwards air force base, then known as Muroc) and at Santa Fé, New Mexico – had tracked the UFO. It had been partially disabled and fell 'dead stick', thus nearly intact. The bodies were taken at first to Edwards air force base and then to Wright Patterson, where they were maintained in cryogenic suspension (and may well still be so). Autopsies had been conducted. They were between 91 and 122 cm (3 and 4 ft) tall, with large heads, slanting eyes and an oriental appearance, but they had normal O type blood and seemed human in most respects!

In 1991, ufologists William Jones and Rebecca Minshall made a very objective attempt to check out the story, which proved enlightening. They drew a blank in Aztec. For example, a deputy sheriff, Wright McEwen, who reputedly fled the crash site in April 1948, confirmed he was there, that he did leave that very month to live in California and that he had heard rumours about the crash. But he emphatically denied any involvement and was sure that no UFO could have crashed without his knowledge. Indeed, nobody in Aztec who was an adult at the time of the alleged events had a positive thing to say about it. The overriding impression was that the story was a myth which nobody knew anything about.

Jones and Minshall also verified that the reputed crash site in Hart Canyon was owned by the government. Some ufologists have considered that important as evidence of the official desire to protect it. However, much of the land is government owned and this parcel had never been in private hands, even before 1948. There were no efforts to stop anyone from doing what they liked at the site, which makes its purchase for sinister reasons less than credible.

The two researchers finally spoke with Francis Broman, the class tutor at Denver University who organized Newton's 1950 lecture. He noted that it was held at 10 am (contrary to what Scully had said), was titled 'Science and Man' and that it was widely known in advance to be about flying saucers; for that reason, over 300 students attended and a larger lecture theatre than originally planned had to be secured. Broman reported that the lecture had been arranged so that his students could practise their 'critical thinking' techniques when faced with a strange story. He agreed that Silas Newton had insisted upon anonymity, for fear of government interest, but added that neither he nor most of the students had found Newton's yarn especially convincing. The oddest aspect of Broman's testimony is that immediately after the lecture a stranger phoned his home about it. Broman had not returned from college by then, but the person called again after his return. It was a man who said he was an intelligence officer (Broman was unclear 40 years on if he had said FBI or air force intelligence). He was only interested in Broman and his students' opinion of the lecturer. Broman replied they had not been convinced and the caller hung up, clearly satisfied with that answer.

This seems to make sense of two FBI memos released almost 30 years later by the FoI act. One is dated 31 March (i.e., three weeks after the lecture) and it had been sent to the FBI director in New Orleans. It tells of how a 'prominent Denver oilman' had been talking about a crashed UFO and its dead occupants for three months. Further, that these beings were 'three foot tall' and the UFO was of 'very hard metal and near indestructible'. In addition, the oilman (obviously Silas Newton) was now reportedly saying that he had received 'telephone calls from Washington DC and from the FBI in which he was requested to keep the information to himself and that, thereafter, he became mysterious about the entire matter.'

The other memo, written nine days earlier, was from FBI agent Guy Hottel in Washington DC and addressed to his director J. Edgar Hoover. It is rather more curious, reporting that 'An investigator for the air force stated that three so-called flying saucers had been recovered in New Mexico.' It added more about the UFOs and the small entities ('dressed in a metallic cloth of a very fine texture'). It also claimed that the 'saucers were found in New Mexico due to the fact that the Government had a very high-powered radar set-up in that area and it is believed the radar interferes with the controlling mechanism of the saucers'. This suggests that the intelligence services were, for some reason, very interested in the response to the claims of Silas Newton. If these were wild fantasies then such interest seems odd, unless they suspected a crime. But there is no evidence that they did. Of course, if the intelligence agencies had helped spin the stories in the first place, as Randle and Schmitt indirectly suggest, perhaps by letting anonymous sources feed false data to 'Dr Gee' and Silas Newton, they would need to monitor the reaction.

However, if someone high up in the government had fears about the Roswell crash getting out, the memos and phone calls fall into place. Perhaps the Aztec story, even if it were a complete hoax, chanced to be too close for comfort to the reality of Roswell. Until it was absolutely clear that the Scully book was not going to lead to the unravelling of that carefully hidden truth, lurking unsuspected behind the weather-balloon cover-up, then a few discreet enquiries may have been thought necessary to make sure . . . If so, the US government was lucky – that time!

1948:
ALIEN DIES IN TEXAS SHOOT-OUT

Probably the most horrendous alien retrieval, or perhaps just the sickest hoax, also dates from 1948. For many years it was inextricably confused with the Aztec affair. However, in 1977 the first hints appeared that there may have been a second alleged incident, near Laredo, Texas. The original source was Todd Zechel, an ex-intelligence officer who had been a prime mover in squeezing out documents from the US government using the FoI Act. Zechel was then with the respected UFO group GSW (Ground Saucer Watch), noted for its demystification of several key photographic cases using sophisticated computer technology. Zechel's source was not immediately promising – the uncle of an anonymous air force technician. The technician had worked at Carswell air force base in Texas, the very same base where Roger Ramey's weather-balloon story was acted out during the Roswell case. At some point in 1948 he had been involved in cordoning off an area on the border between Texas and Mexico, near the town of Laredo. A 27-m (90-ft) diameter disc, which had impacted in the ground, was subsequently recovered. In fact, reputedly, the crash site was 48 km (30 miles) into Mexican territory, but just how the legalities were handled of US troops recovering debris from foreign soil was less than evident at first.

Len Stringfield later learned that there were other witnesses to the alleged crash, in which a hairless entity some 120 cm (4 ft) tall had died. They included a US naval officer, who rushed to the site from Mexico City, only to arrive as the wreckage, covered in canvas, was being taken away on trucks.

The best alleged witness was a USAF captain flying a jet fighter out of Dias air force base in Texas, who saw the object as it zipped past over Albuquerque. It was lost from his radar screen travelling at 3,200 km/hr (2,000 mph) and its impact point plotted. He returned to base and flew out to the crash site in a small aircraft. By the time he and his co-pilot located the debris, a military recovery team was already at work.

In late 1978 Williard McIntyre, Charles Wilhelm and Dennis Pilchis, representing what they called the 'Coalition of Concerned Ufologists of America', released an extraordinary and gruesome photograph. It showed what was indisputably a horribly burned body, with a large head, inside the wreckage of some device. The story that accompanied the picture was about a young naval-photographer who had been taken to Mexico on 7/8 July 1948 in response to reports of a large disc that had crashed just across the border from Laredo. Timothy Green Beckley claimed to have investigated the matter and had communication with the photographer during 1979 and 1980 and, he reports, 'everything checked out exactly as he had said'. The photographer said he was based at White Sands in New Mexico and his normal job was to photograph plane crashes to allow experts to look for signs of metal fatigue. He had also filmed the aftermath of nuclear tests in New Mexico.

At 1.22 pm, an object was tracked on radar, heading at great speed from the west coast towards Texas. It was intercepted above Albuquerque just after 2 pm, by two jets from Dias air force base, one of them presumably flown by the pilot mentioned above. The object then supposedly changed direction (possibly it was fired upon?) and was seen to be wobbling in flight. At about 2.30 it had reduced speed to under 160 km/hr (100 mph) and it disappeared off the radar screens near the Texas/Mexico border, at a point, located by plotting reports from several radar stations, near the Sabinas River.

The Mexican government was advised of the incident, and a US investigation team went to the site that same evening. The naval photographer and four colleagues were alerted around 8 pm and flown to Del Rio, Texas, where their aircraft refuelled and flew on to the site. They arrived there after 2 am, to be told that they were to film the crash of a top-secret, experimental aircraft. The object was badly damaged and still smouldering when they reached it. It looked like an earthly craft and even had what appeared to be nuts and bolts, but these had to be broken off because they could not be undone. Diamond drills had to be used to break the very hard metal. At the crash scene, there was also some thin foil, like cigarette paper, but extremely tough, which was collected up by military police. Later, a metallurgist was heard to say that the craft was made of an alloy, with a honeycomb lattice that contained silicon, but that was as much as he could figure out.

The body was inside the wreckage and it was filmed, illuminated by arc lights, despite the heat still being given off. The body was 1.4 m (4 ft 6 in) tall, with a large head and huge, round eye sockets. Its hands were claw-like, with only four fingers' and the arms were very long. Allegedly, two army doctors arrived at dawn and conducted an examination of the body after it was pulled from the craft. The photographer heard them discuss some things. For instance, the skin was said to be grey and smooth, rather of the texture of a woman's breasts. There was no sign of muscles, their function being carried out by a very intricate network of bones. There was no sign of blood, only a slight green fluid with a strong smell of sulphur. The body also showed no indication of hair growth; nor were there any obvious sexual organs. The photographer and his assistants took 500 pictures of the body and wreckage. By the time they were flown out of the area, early in the afternoon, trucks, including some from the Mexican government apparently, were taking the debris away, heading for Monterey.

All the photographs were processed under strict secrecy and the matter was hushed up. Only years later, when the photographer left his base and the story still had not emerged, did he make duplicate negatives of 40 of the pictures and take them with him. Then, when the dust had settled and 30 years had passed, he chose to make a few of them available, and most were eventually seen by ufologists. Analysis of the negatives by Kodak showed that they had probably been processed 30 years earlier, fitting the evidence. Ground Saucer Watch carried out computer enhancement and concurred with this. Without knowing the story of the photographer, a trained medical expert commented that signs of rigor mortis were visible on the body, indicating death about 12 hours previously, which exactly matched the witness's testimony. However, lest you think that this UFO group was affirming the reality of the photographs, it was not: it concluded that the entity on the film was a primate, perhaps a monkey or orang-utan.

As mentioned in the previous chapter, the Americans test-flew V-rockets and in 1948 at least one went awry and crash-landed in Mexico. Also, not long after July 1948, monkeys were sometimes used as 'pilots' in early space rocket experiments. Hence, most UFO researchers believe that the crash story is probably accurate and that the rumours about aliens merely grew up as a result of speculation (and may even have been allowed to develop to protect what was really happening). The photographer and his team were flown out to record the accident in what would have been, just as they were told, a very top secret experimental mission, especially given the involvement of Mexican territory. No doubt the Mexican government had been primed by American officials to co-operate in their crashed rocket's recovery. However, there are some who think this was not a monkey-piloted V rocket, noting in particular the fact that the wreckage more resembles the cockpit of an aircraft than a V-2 rocket. Moreover, there is clear evidence of what looks like the frames of a pair of spectacles or sunglasses within the twisted metal. As monkeys do not wear these, that rather implies that the victim may have been a human pilot killed in a terrible inferno after an experimental aircraft went down. Of course, this has not utterly scotched the rumours that the Laredo alien really is an extraterrestrial shot from the skies after a confrontation with the USAF. Frankly, if the photographer's story is completely credible, then that would be the only possible explanation, because there are parts of his story which simply do not fit other options. Opinion is divided, but few ufologists openly contend that these photographs are strong proof of an alien-retrieval operation.

CHAPTER FOUR

WHAT GOES UP, MUST COME DOWN

The 1950s were an exciting decade. The excesses of war were cast off as just a bad memory and the technology that had been used to annihilate millions quickly found a new home as a worker of miracles. Nowhere was this more evident than in the dawn of space flight, using old war-time rockets. From the then highly advanced Nazi V-rockets and the Cold War race to build intercontinental missiles came the quest to reach earth orbit with a human payload. A battle royal took place between the Americans and the USSR, which, initially at least, it seemed that the Russians had won.

Certainly, the USSR was the first to launch an orbiting space craft (*Sputnik* in 1957) and soon after became the first to get a man beyond the pull of earth's gravity, when Uri Gagarin wrote his name into the history books with his epic flight. But the primitive nature of the Soviet technology had its toll, with crashes and accidents kept secret from even the USSR's own people until very recently. And so the Americans' slow-but-steady approach paid off in the end. They were not to be free of tragedy either, but by the early 1960s they had a clear lead in the race to get a man on the moon.

Accompanying all this excitement was a new-found interest in space fiction. Movies in particular played a strong part and took little time to incorporate UFOs into their plot lines. The discovery of a crashed UFO buried in the frozen Arctic wastes formed the basis for the chilling movie, *The Thing from Another World* (remade as just *The Thing* in 1982). Premiered in 1951, the film pre-empted by just a few months the first, rather similar, case discussed below; whether or not this was a coincidence is open to conjecture. In *The Day the Earth Stood Still*, the idea of UFOs stalling car engines – a frequent feature of real close encounters – was first dramatized. However, none of these movies, or the radio and TV serials that hooked millions on to a fascination with space, was in any sense a *real* UFO story. The portrayal of reality as reality was still many years away.

During the 1950s the UFO mystery went through an uneasy

transition. The first UFO groups were set up. About 20 serious books appeared, notably the 1956 memoirs of the head of the USAF intelligence team at Wright Patterson in Dayton, Ohio. This devastating document, *The Report on Unidentified Flying Objects* by Lieutenant Edward Ruppelt, was the first truly important UFO publication, and it remains a classic. Ruppelt braved the wrath of his former employers by telling it as he saw it – that is, that, despite the cover-up, some UFOs were truly baffling phenomena; but it contained nothing about Roswell, other UFO crashes, or their retrieved occupants, even though some other secret data were touched upon. Possibly, as Ruppelt himself speculated in the book, he was 'just the front man', acting as a scapegoat for public and media anger against air force inefficiency; the true UFO study went on way above him.

During the 1950s ufologists also had to contend with much ridicule because of the contactee movement – a number of individuals who wrote best-selling books and launched semi-religious cults. They professed contact with friendly 'space brothers' from Venus and other planets, which had the effect of switching many (including UFO researchers) away from any interest in the pilots who might have flown the flying saucers. The contactees never described the small, egg-headed, large-eyed aliens repeatedly alleged to have been seen at crash sites mentioned in this book. Instead they were always much more human-like and, frankly, pretty unalien and incredible. Even Ruppelt was so concerned by the way the public took to their tales that he issued a revised edition of his own book a couple of years after it first appeared and not long before he died, tragically young. In effect, he withdrew all suggestion that UFOs were now a serious problem and privately cited the contactee movement as the cause of his disenchantment.

There are some people who think Ruppelt was 'persuaded' to change his mind because his book was proving too influential. There are others who think one or two key contactee stories were planted by intelligence agencies as a deliberate ploy to limit interest in aliens. This may have reduced the chance of actual retrievals coming out into the open . . . We may never know.

1952:
EUROPE'S FIRST RETRIEVAL

On 23 May 1955 various newspapers syndicated a column by
Dorothy Kilgallen, one of America's top European correspon-
dents, based in London. Her story was so remarkable that it
burst through the barriers of disbelief and got some (albeit limited) mention in the third issue of *Flying Saucer Review*, later
that year.

Kilgallen alleged that she had discovered how 'British scientists and airmen' had had access to 'the wreckage of one
mysterious flying ship' and had thus concluded from their
analysis that they were 'flying saucers which originate on
another world'. The journalist, who freely circulated among
many high rollers in society, stated that her anonymous source
was from the British government and of 'Cabinet rank'.
Moreover, she claimed that the investigation had shown that
'the saucers were staffed by small men – probably under four
feet tall.'

Of course, in 1955 there was no context of Roswell, Aztec,
Laredo, etc., into which to slot this new story. While small
beings had been reported in UFO cases – notably the wave of
alien contacts in France during October 1954 – they were virtually unknown in Britain, where tall, blond-haired entities
were almost exclusively the order of the day. Indeed, the contactee movement was so influential in 1955 that most people
would have considered these small entities absurd, rather than
the norm, which movies and books from the 1980s and 1990s
may have made this description seem to be. That alone may be
sufficient ground to take this story seriously, even without
Kilgallen's impeccable record. She never retracted the report,
but she also never elaborated upon it. Various attempts to verify it – for example, by British researcher Tim Good – all failed.
According to *Flying Saucer Review*, one source indicated that
Lord Louis Mountbatten was the originator of the story. He
certainly had an interest in UFOs (as do his relatives in the
British royal family). But his association with Kilgallen's
scoop is really just conjecture. People suggest that whoever
told these things to her (allegedly at a cocktail party) may
have intended them as a joke. Maybe so, but if these words
were spoken in jest, then it is interesting how well they fit the
knowledge that was then unknown but which we now possess

about crashed UFOs – or, in fact, match the following case.

In June 1952 stories had circulated in the German Press about a remarkable incident on the island of Spitsbergen, a remote, rocky outcrop off the northern coast of Norway, on the very edge of the polar regions. Researcher Ole Jonny Braenne has found that the earliest known mention of the incident was 28 June. In this account the *Saarbrucker Zeitung* reported how Norwegian jets were on a summer exercise (dates between late May and mid-June have been cited in various sources), when six of them flew over Spitsbergen in search of their practice target aircraft. As they crossed the Hinlopen Straits, intense static hampered radio contact between the aircraft. About the same time, the radar at Narvik, their home base on the Norwegian mainland, was showing a distorted signal of the jet fighters, as well as the presence of a UFO emitting unknown radio frequencies – presumably the source of the interference.

While the jets were circling the island, Flight Captain Olaf Larsen spotted a large metallic disc in the snow. It had clearly crashed and was badly damaged, but it was relatively intact. After ensuring there was no sign of a crew, the jets returned to Narvik to file a report. By the end of that day, several ski-fitted flying-boats had located the wreckage and landed on the icy waters alongside it.

The 45-m (150-ft) diameter craft was embedded in several metres of snow and ice. Dr Norsel, said to be a Norwegian rocket scientist, flew with the recovery team and discovered that a radioactive unit in the craft was emitting energy at the frequency of 934 Hertz. It had probably been the cause of the radio and radar malfunctions. The craft itself was made of an 'unknown metal', silver in colour, and it was powered by a ring of jets on the underside. Symbols on the inside of the device were foreign (thought to be similar to the Russian Cyrillic alphabet). No crew seemd to be present and everyone speculated that it was a prototype, remote-controlled Soviet aircraft of very advanced design. It was planned to ship the wreckage to Narvik.

While this story had a brief mention in the German Press in 1952, it was not until July 1954 before any fuller details were reported. Then the *Hessische Nachrichten* described the results of the long investigation headed by a Colonel Gernod Darnhyl. This was to turn the case on its head. Darnhyl alleged that the original view – that the UFO was a version of a Nazi prototype developed by the Soviets – had proven to be in error. In fact, the disc had 'emphatically – not been built by any country on earth', he said; for a start, the metal of which the craft was made could not be identified. Darnhyl also noted that both the Americans and the British had been brought into the investigation (indeed later stories referred to the idea that the UFO, or parts of it, had been shipped to Britain for a more thorough examination after the Norwegian appraisal failed to find any explanation). This makes sense, for we know that what was at first (wrongly) assumed to be V-rocket debris found in Scandinavia in 1946 was sent to the British authorities for further testing. Was this 1952 crash the 'British' UFO that Dorothy Kilgallen referred to soon afterwards? Another claim was that Norwegian pilots had regularly patrolled the polar latitudes between 1952 and 1954, looking for evidence of further flights. They had often seen UFOs in the skies.

From this point on, it is difficult to tell where informed comment ended and speculation began. Further stories spoke of the craft's metal being unusually light, like aluminium, yet incredibly strong and impervious to tests. It was even said that two men could lift the huge disc up by one of its sides, so light was the metal. A report from South America referred to burnt bodies being found inside the wreckage, but this was never confirmed.

Again, you will notice the Roswell features of unusual lettering (hieroglyphics, Cyrillic alphabet, Japanese picture language, etc.) inside the craft and again this same thin, incredibly resilient yet light-weight metal. Given that these consistencies were not at all obvious even to UFO researchers by 1955, their recurrence is intriguing. Equally interesting is that Alan Harbinson admits that his 1980 novel, *Genesis*, was based upon research into renegade Nazis developing flying saucers at a polar base. Although the Spitsbergen story does not feature in Harbinson's factual afterword, its potential relevance is clear.

In 1990, Bill Moore, the American who had devoted much time to the Roswell case, described a recent visit to Europe. French researcher Jean Sider had shown him a report that he had uncovered from *Le Lorain* (a newspaper in Nancy), dated 15 October 1954. It added a new twist to the Spitsbergen story. The newspaper said a Swiss Air Defence unit had investigated the Spitsbergen affair as part of a general study into UFOs. It reported the claim that the Nazis had built and test-flown a circular craft from the Harz Mountains on 14 February 1945 and added further details that matched the original Spitsbergen story – for instance, that it had jets on the underside, set in a circle, to propel the craft skyward. It is worth noting that in the late 1950s some prototype circular jet craft were built in North America, for instance, the one by AV Roe of Canada, which was very like a flying saucer in design. Two of these were tested by the US military before 1960 but, reportedly, they barely flew and were so unstable that the project was scrapped. They used a similar principle to that reputedly tried more successfully by the Nazis in 1945 and, perhaps, by whoever flew the Spitsbergen saucer seven years later.

So, is the Spitsbergen crash another myth? Or, did it really happen and was it the result of a secret prototype jet aircraft that crashed during an unmanned flight in this remote area, far from prying eyes? To be truthful, both these possibilities cannot be rejected, given what we know and, since none of the original sources is available for interview, any other conclusion is unlikely to be established. Randle and Schmitt note that the USAF archives claim that their UFO investigation team was satisfied as early as September 1952 that the story was a hoax. While we cannot say with assurance that this might not have been Europe's first taste of a genuine alien retrieval, that prospect is far from established by these skimpy, largely unauthenticated facts.

1953:
A CRASH IN CANYON-LAND

Kingman, Arizona, sits amid rugged desert terrain, just south of the spectacular natural beauty of the Grand Canyon. Here, a UFO is rumoured to have crashed just before 20 May 1953. It is possibly America's second most documented retrieval story, but it certainly has less hard evidence to support it than the Roswell affair.

It was first clearly described to the respected ufologist Ray Fowler in June 1973 by a witness referred to as 'Fritz Werner', who even signed a legal affidavit vouching to the honesty of his testimony. Do not forget that 1973 predates the modern rediscovery of the Roswell affair. Werner said he had been working on a special contract at a nuclear test site in Nevada, assessing blast damage to structures after explosions. He was

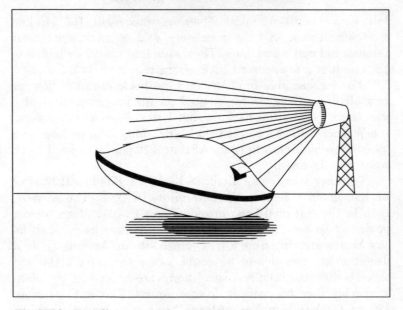

*The UFO allegedly seen on the ground at Kingman, Arizona,
in May 1953.*

called away by the scientist leading the team and told that he
was to go on special duty on 21 May. So he was flown by military aircraft to Phoenix and then taken (he thinks) north-west
in a bus, with blacked-out windows. Werner was ordered not
to talk to anybody else during the journey.

After four hours, the 16 passengers reached the crash site
and, amid tight security, they were allowed to see a 9-m (30-ft)
diameter disc embedded in the sand for about 50 cm (20 in) at
an acute angle. It was illuminated by very strong arc-lights
and seemed to be constructed of aluminium-like metal. It
appeared relatively undamaged. A small, open hatchway was
visible. Werner was given the task of estimating the impact
speed of the craft from the evidence available. Once he had
done so, he was interviewed on tape and escorted back to the
bus. He talked with one of the other members of the team, who
spoke of seeing a small cabin with chairs inside, before the two
men were quickly separated. Any questions not relevant to
Werner's work were ignored by the USAF colonel in charge of
the operations.

Before being made to sign an oath of secrecy and led away,
Werner claims he sneaked a look inside a well-guarded tent.
There he saw briefly the body of an entity about 120 cm (4 ft)

tall, with a skull-cap and a silver, one-piece suit. Its skin had a brownish cast. All the men were told to hand-write their reports and make no copies. They were told that they had seen the crash of a top-secret USAF aircraft.

Fowler was able to check into the background of Werner and all his colleagues commented on his integrity. He had a very strong scientific background. Later, Fowler was able to see Werner's diary and read that on 21 May 1953 he had been 'picked up at Indian Springs AFB at 4.30 pm for a job I can't write or talk about'.

Another story came direct to Len Stringfield in 1977 after he had given a lecture to some pilots in Ohio. The witness, then in the National Guard, told of how in 1953 ('I am almost positive') he was at Wright Patterson air force base, when he saw crates arriving from a UFO crash site in 'Arizona . . . in a desert area' (the closest he could locate the event). He said three bodies had been recovered and were packed in dry ice in a special way to prevent freezer burns. The entities were 120 cm (4 ft) tall, with over-large heads and brownish skins. One appeared to be female. Of the wreckage, he referred to symbols inside it which he described as being akin to 'Sanskrit'. However, his exposure to the debris was very limited. This witness would not break his oath of secrecy to write an account, but he tried to get permission to leave a written statement to be opened after his death. This was officially denied him in emphatic terms. Later he moved away with his family without leaving a forwarding address, after having previously been very open and co-operative with Stringfield.

An almost identical story was reported to ufologist Charles Wilhelm in 1966 by a man who said that his father had told it to him as a death-bed confession. The description of the body, the dating of the year as 1953, and his placement at Wright Patterson when the wreckage arrived, all matched.

However, the earliest reference seems to have been made to MUFON researcher Richard Hall in April 1964. He was told the story by a future Vietnam commander about whom, Hall said, 'I could not imagine a less likely hoaxer.' This man was reputedly advised of the news by his air force training officer. He spoke about a 1953 crash in the Arizona area from which four small bodies were recovered. The descriptions of the craft and of the bodies were, again, extraordinarily consistent.

These accounts are certainly all circumstantial, usually also second-hand. However, they seem to be completely independent of one another and require consideration if only because of the many parallels. The Kingman, Arizona, case may simply be an example of what the Roswell affair would have been like had no wreckage been found by a civilian and had not the crucial initial error been made to issue a Press release. Perhaps it, too, would only have surfaced in a series of interlocking rumours and belated stories from obviously bemused, but equally, concerned scientists and air force personnel. We are left, then, not to know, but to surmise.

1955:
AN ALIEN'S DYING WORDS

The sighting of a crashing UFO is, unsurprisingly, very rare. However, according to an amazing, if unsupportable, story from John La Fontaine, he has met a man who professed to witness exactly that in July 1955.

The event was reported by the witness during a UFO slide show in Copenhagen. The man told La Fontaine that he had been working as a lumberjack in Vestra Norrland, Sweden. Around 6 am, he and two other men (brothers) were felling trees when a cigar-shaped object crossed the sky, obviously in difficulty. Thinking it was an aircraft, they rushed towards what would be its impact point and, expecting to hear a terrible crash, were instead greeted only with a blinding, but silent, flash of light. Moments later, everything was sucked towards the light. The lumberjacks were thrown to the ground, as branches and other forest debris flew past them. The suction effect was very brief, but strong enough to pull the witness painfully into the base of a tree. Recovering and then going to the clearing where the impact had occurred, the three shaken lumberjacks were amazed to find nothing there, save a prone figure seemingly dead. They assumed that the craft had fallen into a nearby river and that the person had managed to eject from it.

However, the figure was not dead. As one of the three men went to touch him, he backed off, in pain, saying in perfect Swedish that he felt as if he had been struck by an electric shock, and he urged them to keep away from him. The figure was only about 120 cm (4 ft) tall, with a large head covered with faint, downy, white hair. A glowing aura surrounded his body, but his skin was yellowish-brown and overall he had a vaguely oriental appearance. By some kind of mental process, he made two of the witnesses leave the scene, but the third stayed for two hours as the aura gradually faded and the figure died. The figure spoke of how several alien races visited the earth to do a range of things; some were just passing through to a parallel universe! The final, enigmatic words of the dying alien were, reputedly, 'You have come without any wish to and depart against your own wish. Our life is like vapour.' Soon afterwards the aura extinguished. As requested, La Fontaine's witness took the sulphurous-smelling body to the river, where it quickly 'dissolved' in a chemical reaction as had been promised.

1957:
BITS OF SPACESHIP RAIN OVER BRAZIL

In possibly the only case of its kind, parts of an alien space-craft were supposedly captured in September 1957 from the beach at Ubatuba, Brazil. They represent the one and only chance we have had so far, in civilian life, to conduct laboratory analysis on what are potentially alien metal fragments from a crashed UFO.

The story began with a letter, received on 13 September by Ibrahim Sued, a columnist with *O Globo*, one of Brazil's leading newspapers that had often featured UFO stories. The letter was published in the newspapers the next day. The letter was signed, but its signature was unreadable. It said that at noon on 10 September, the writer and several friends were fishing near Ubatuba in São Paulo state, when a disc-shaped craft appeared in the sky. It was heading towards the beach at great speed, and almost certain to crash. However, before disaster struck, it made a sharp upward turn, as if pulling out of the dive, and climbed at terrific speed almost vertically. Moments later, it exploded in a huge flash of light and 'disintegrated into thousands of fiery fragments which fell sparkling with magnificent brightness. They looked like fireworks.' Most of the wreckage plunged into the sea, but a few bits fell on the beach and the fishermen rushed to them. The pieces were small, but were remarkably light – 'as light as paper', even for the largest bits. The letterwriter concluded his account by say-

ing, 'I enclose herewith a small sample . . . I do not know anyone that could be trusted to whom I might send it for analysis.'

While Sued liked the story, one of Brazil's top UFO
experts, whom he contacted about it, was not impressed
because none of the witnesses was traceable. Dr Olavo Fontes,
a respected doctor with government connections, initially
assumed that the story was probably a hoax. Nevertheless, he
agreed to check it out and soon came to change his opinion.
Fontes was associated with the American UFO group APRO
(Aerial Phenomena Research Organization). Two of the three
samples sent to Sued were sent off to APRO in New Mexico.
The third one was retained by Fontes for study in Brazil.

At first glance, the three samples looked like pieces of
irregular and highly oxidized metal, coloured dull whitish-
grey. They did look like fragments from something that had
broken up in an explosion, thus matching the witnesses' otherwise unverifiable story. Unfortunately, the handling of this
precious evidence by the analysts was often problematic and
caused more confusion than resolution. The first piece was
tested at the mineral production labs in the Brazilian agricul-
tural ministry. They applied chemical, spectrographic analysis
and X-ray diffusion techniques on the 'alien' metal. These
quickly established that the fragment was very pure magnesium. Indeed, chemist Luisa Barbosa noted that the normal
trace elements expected in magnesium were all missing.
Magnesium burns fiercely with a brilliant white flame and
rapidly oxidizes in air, as the witnesses' testimony, but it was
hardly the best material for a spaceship hull! Fontes used up
all of his sample in an array of further tests, which included
another chemist conducting a spectrographic analysis and X-
ray investigation at the crystallography labs of a geology unit
and pieces even being taken to the Brazilian Army and Navy
research departments. The latter two kept their findings
secret, but the geology unit's report broadly supported the first
one. The sample was magnesium of surprising purity and a
density of 1.87 – higher than the normal 1.74. If these findings
could be replicated in the USA with the other two samples,
then the possibility of an exciting breakthrough was evident.

APRO was in no doubt and in early 1960 informed the
USAF that it had bits of a spaceship 'which met disaster in the
earth's atmosphere'. Bits of the samples were unselfishly sent
to the USAF for their own investigation. Regrettably the air
force technician destroyed it by accident as he prepared to

start his readings. The USAF requested a replacement to continue their work; not surprisingly, APRO declined!

Another test at the Atomic Energy Commission plant had found the density of one of the APRO samples to be 1.75, almost exactly normal and not the extraordinarily high figure claimed for the fragment tested in Brazil. The high density reading might have been due to the oxidization of the metal.

In 1968, when the US government funded a team of scientists at the University of Colorado to study UFOs, APRO was persuaded to allow some of its sample to be removed from a bank vault and handed over to the government investigators. Chemist Dr Roy Craig was put in charge and published a report on his enquiries as part of the so-called 'Condon Report' in January 1969. Craig employed the laboratories of the Alcohol and Tobacco Tax division in Washington, because of their ability to record small amounts of impurities. Samples of manufactured magnesium from the Dow company were used as a comparison. The tests discovered that, while the sample was quite pure magnesium, it was nothing like as pure as the Brazilian one. Moreover, the impurities were not unusual, save one, strontium. Yet, despite Dow thinking that nobody would intentionally add this element to processed magnesium, they found that they themselves had once done so experimentally. In fact, they had produced material like the Ubutuba fragment back in 1940, which had almost the same quantity of strontium in it. Craig also reported that the magnesium showed no signs of having been interfered with structurally, since it had crystallized. This implied that nobody had used it in the construction of an aircraft; although that, of course, was applying the logic of earthly construction techniques.

Unsurprisingly, the Condon team concluded that, despite APRO's claims for the fragments, they represented no evidence of anything fantastic: they were just fairly ordinary bits of magnesium that any hoaxer could have obtained with little effort. However, one Condon team member pointed out that the most interesting feature of the sample was the missing trace elements (calcium, for example) which were normally present in earthly magnesium. They were not found even by Craig's detailed investigation. That was a mystery. APRO fought back. They employed Dr Walter Walker, a metallurgist at the University of Arizona, to conduct new tests on their remaining fragment. They had his results independently verified by another scientist, Dr Robert Johnson, at a materials research laboratory in New Jersey. These two scientists reached similar conclusions, but very different from those of the Condon team. They believed that the magnesium had undergone a special type of process to control the directional growth of the metal crystals. However, this form of artificial technique was unknown in 1957 and was only just under development by 1969. Intriguingly, directional crystallization produces materials tough enough to withstand re-entry into the atmosphere! The scientists did warn about the small size of the sample being tested and pointed out that, although their results implied it was a piece from a larger, probably manufactured, object, they could not say what type of object this might have been. Controversy thus raged around their results.

One final investigation – by industrial chemist and Australian ufologist Bill Chalker – used 1980s techniques to discover the precise isotopes of magnesium to be found within the final, fast-dwindling sample. He found that, while they were fairly unusual, they were not unearthly and so, again, this work offered no real support for the extraterrestrial origin of the Ubutuba-like fragment. Without more evidence to support the case, it will probably always remain controversial and unprovable.

1957:
SCARBOROUGH FLAIR

Of all the resting places for a crashed spaceship, probably the least likely to spring to mind is an unidentified 'fish and chip shop somewhere in east Yorkshire'. But that is the apparent location for the UK's first undisputed crashed saucer, according to rumour and legend, that is. That no secret agents have yet been to retrieve it and send its remains for analysis to the legendary Hangar 18 at Wright Patterson Air Force base, probably supports the common perception that the case was just a hoax. But what a hoax! If this affair were a mere jest, then it shows the UK's ingenuity (and off-the-wall sense of humour) at its very best.

The story begins on 21 November 1957, when three men were driving up Rcasty Hill, part of the wild Silpho Moor, north-west of the seaside resort of Scarborough in north Yorkshire. They were not far from the notorious Fylingdales radar station, where huge golf balls dominated the bleak Cold War terrain as part of NATO's early-warning system against nuclear attack. The men were the driver, Frank Dickenson (sometimes also called Frank Hutton), and Fred Taylor and Charles Thomas. Some sources allege these names could be fictitious. It was late evening and, while climbing up the hill, the car's engine began to falter, rapidly bringing the vehicle to a halt. Outside, Frank had seen a round glow which seemed to hover at the side of the road and then crash on to the moors. The glow seemed to appear at the same time as the engine faltered. Charles Thomas, in the back seat, reported later that he saw a brief flare of light in the sky at this time that resembled a meteor. Fred Taylor, in the passenger seat, evidently saw nothing at all.

Frank grabbed a flashlight and left the car, handbrake on, to scramble up the rough heather slope. Neither of the other men was willing to risk the rough gorse in the pitch blackness. At the top of the rise, and only 30 m (100 ft) or so from the stalled car, Frank found a small saucer-shaped device embedded loosely in the ground. Standing beside it was a man and woman who had evidently seen the thing crash just as he had done. After exchanging a few words with them, Frank scuttled down the incline and more or less dragged his two companions back up the hill. But when they reached the spot, neither the couple nor the UFO were to be seen. Unsurprisingly, Frank's companions would not accept his story. They drove around in the dark for a while, searching for either the UFO or the mysterious couple, then gave up. However, Frank was determined to prove his case and put an appeal in the personal column of the Scarborough evening paper, urging the strangers to come forward and speak up.

They did. Or at least, Frank was later called by someone professing to be the man he had met on the moors, stating firmly that he now had the UFO at his home. However, he recognized that Frank had a right of co-ownership and offered to let him visit and take a look at this prize possession. This was unsatisfactory to Frank, who wanted to own the thing exclusively. So he offered a couple of pounds for the privilege. The sharp man, who had previously expressed little obvious interest in the object, now said, 'If you want it that bad, it must be worth something!' As a result, there was some haggling and Frank eventually offered a price (reputedly £10) which was accepted. In 1957 terms that was a tidy sum.

The exchange followed soon after, at an agreed spot. No words were spoken and Frank handed over the money and received the crashed UFO inside an old sack. Delighted with this purchase, the amateur ufologist set about analysing it and bringing the story to the attention of a few local reporters. However, it never seems to have gone much beyond that. According to ufologist Roger Ford, who in 1990 claimed to have known personally one of the three men in the car, this was partly because the British government had reputedly issued a 'D' notice. (A 'D' – for Defence–notice is a way the UK press can be prevented from printing stories which the authorities prefer not to appear, citing national security implications.) At first, Frank was concerned that his UFO might be radioactive, so he visited a local science writer, who suggested a test. An unexposed roll of film was left with the UFO inside the sack for four days and then processed. Had the object been radioactive, then the film would have been fogged. It was not, so the device was pronounced safe. At this point, my contact, Dr John Dale (a clinical psychologist), became involved. In 1957 John was a member of the Stockport-based UFO group DIGAP (Direct Investigation Group into Aerial Phenomena), one of the oldest in the world. He visited Frank and filmed the object both before and after Frank began the next phase – to dissect it!

According to photographs (which I have seen) and Dr Dale's investigations at the time, the object was a classic saucer shape, with a slightly conical base. It was made of dark metal and seemed well machined. The top was coated in white plastic. The underside appeared to be like copper. Overall it was 46 cm (18 in) in diameter and 23 cm (9 in) deep. It weighed about 16 kg (35 lb). After opening it up, Frank discovered a hollow copper rod from the base to the top. A metal coil was wrapped tightly around it and a series of hieroglyphic symbols were etched into the side. Inside the tube were 17 very thin, interlocking copper-foil sheets, which were covered with similar hieroglyphics.

The pattern of Roswell, Kingman, Spitsbergen, etc., was being repeated, yet again, with this set of symbols. However, unlike those cases, this was very obviously not a piloted craft, unless the occupants were *very* little green men, considerably under the usual 120 cm (4 ft)! There was no obvious sign of a propulsion system, save the coil and tube which seemed to signify nothing in particular. This was, however, to be

Some of the hieroglyphics found etched inside the Silpho Moor saucer, in November 1957.

elaborated upon later (in the decoded text) as a magnetic propulsion drive.

Dr Dale arranged for a metallurgist at Manchester University to study the disc. The man refused to be identified, but his report (which I have seen) stated that the object was primarily lead, as used in industrial bearings. The copper foil was triple laminated (a common industrial process) and contained less than 5 per cent iron. The symbols were etched into this with a metal stylus. The metallurgist tested the metal and was adamant that it could not have been exposed to air above a temperature of 150°C (320°F). Thus, he was convinced that it could not possibly have come from space because it had not encountered the high temperatures of the earth's atmosphere. However, his report also noted that the copper was unusually pure and that the normal tin and nickel impurity content (in one part per ten thousand) was completely absent from the sample within this disc. This is rather reminiscent of the Ubutuba affair which, of course, predated this incident by only a matter of weeks. In conclusion, the metallurgist noted that the device was the result of quite complex and skilled work and would have cost whoever had built it considerably more than the £10 Frank Dickenson reportedly paid. Indeed, in modern terms it would probably take a four-figure sum to reproduce the same kind of object. In other words, this was no casual hoaxer's effort, thrown together one night at the back of the garage.

Dr Dale then proceeded to have the hieroglyphics decoded. A language expert at Manchester University found this no serious challenge, because it utilized a moderately simple code in which various phonetic sounds matched the orientation of one repeated T symbol drawn at different angles within a circle. As a result, the disc was found to contain an astonishing 2,000-word message, reportedly penned by an alien calling himself 'Ullo', although with some text later added by an (apparently female) colleague called 'Tarngee'. The text begins with, 'I write this message to you my friends on the planet of the sun

you call earth (*sic*).' Elsewhere in the message we are told that
all the stories from the (then rampant) contactees were hoaxes
and that, as yet, no real contact between aliens and humans
has taken place. Earth folk were warned that they could not
travel into space any distance themselves because of the speeds
of acceleration necessary, which were fatal to human bodies.
The entities describe themselves as 183 cm (6 ft) tall, with
blond hair and blue eyes. But the language struggles at times.
They justify this by saying, 'Our council doesn't want us to
communicate because we are a happy race. Even to contact
your race mentally affects us . . . we have seen your television
and listened to spelling competitions on radio' – but still, it
seems, they cannot grasp the English language and its 'peculiar spelling'. The UFO was reputedly 'an old damaged space
probe vehicle' which they 'alter to land without signals from
ground – this will cause vehicle to crash'. They insist, 'this is
not toy message from one of your people.' This was apparently
a renegade mission, because their 'council' had seen the war-
like ways of the earth and our misuse of atomic power ('Our
recording vehicles on return sometimes found to have atoms
radiating'). So they preferred to wait until conditions got better, because 'You will improve or disappear.'

Interestingly, there are various attempts at humour which
seem rather too 'earthly'. For instance, Tarngee speaks of how
there are 'four women for every man' on their world, making
this seem like a crude male fantasy, but noting enigmatically,
'This is no reason to remove clothes to find measures.'
Elsewhere, they refer to primitive rock music, saying that
'some is better than we can make' but 'much is howling as in
pain'. And that is more or less that. The whereabouts of the
saucer, after about 1960, are lost from ufology, save the story
about its display at a fish and chip shop. It was widely rejected as a joke.

According to Roger Ford, the widow of one of the three
men probably still has the device without realizing what it is.
He claims that, while he owned it, Frank Dickenson's house
suffered poltergeist attacks. Ford also indirectly refers to visi-
tations by strange 'men in black', often deemed to be government agents snooping after information.

Of course, this case is almost certainly an elaborate hoax.
But it was well done. The message is sophisticated and it has
a curious match with another case that occurred the same
week. In that incident (which began only three days before the

alleged crash on Silpho Moor, but was not publicized for some weeks), a woman in Birmingham began to receive a long series of visits from aliens nearly identical to the Silpho Moor message writers. They professed to come from 'Gharnasvarn', offered messages similar to those in the Silpho Moor mini-saucer and generally behaved in a way that made people conclude that these seemingly independent cases were connected. A full account of the Birmingham case appears in *The Complete Book of UFOs*.

At least these alien messages were superior to that left in a field some 30 years later, amid the not-so-mysterious wheat circles. The would-be aliens used such bad grammar that they wrote, 'We are not alone', when, had they been anything but humans talking to one another, they should, of course, have said '*You* are not alone'!

1959:
A POLISH CRASH RETRIEVAL

Little is known about this case, apart from a report by Ion Hobana, a Romanian science writer, and Julien Weverbergh, a Belgian publisher. They presented details in 1972 in their evaluation of media stories and rumours to glean secret data behind the Iron Curtain. From Press accounts from Poland, Hobana and Weverbergh allege that on 21 February 1959 dockside workers at Gdynia saw a glowing mass fall from the sky and crash into the harbour. Three divers were sent into the freezing water by the port authorities and they struggled to find any wreckage in the thick mud. Eventually, they came to the surface with a piece of metal that was seemingly unaffected by its time in the water. It seemed very odd indeed.

Both the Polish Navy and Gdynia University analysed the metal, but no details of their reports were released. There is speculation that the debris might have been from a Soviet space launch experiment that went wrong, because it is now known that several disasters were kept quiet. However, Hobana and Weverbergh also found an alleged sequel to this episode, reputedly a few days after the crash, when members of a patrol guarding the Gdynia coast saw a humanoid figure dragging itself out of the sea, on to the beach, apparently exhausted. How different the entity was from humans was never elaborated, except to say that it did not have the same number of fingers as we do and some of the body organs were unusual. It was also badly burnt, seemingly from a crash. The entity did not respond to any attempted contact. It wore a one-piece, metallic uniform that could not be removed because it had no seams or zippers. It also wore a sort of armband. When this was taken off, the being's health quickly deteriorated, and it soon died. The remains were sent to Moscow for further investigation. Unsurprisingly, nothing further has ever been reported about the matter.

CHAPTER FIVE

THE SPACE AGE

When the history of the twentieth century is told, there is little doubt that the 1960s will be regarded as the space generation, for during that decade just about everything imaginable took place up there. Humankind floated weightless in earth orbit and, after a series of extraordinary adventures pre-scripted by Jules Verne, landed on the moon in July 1969. The high drama of this period did not fail to enthuse people everywhere. Billions tuned into the Apollo missions on TV. Talking about space became commonplace. Alongside the factual excitement came TV series and movies so compulsive that their appeal still endures decades later. The amazing combination of space fiction and movie magic in *2001: A Space Odyssey* and the eternally youthful *Star Trek*, first aired in the nine months running up to the pioneering lunar touchdown, are the most famous media spin offs.

Paradoxically, interest in UFOs went through what has been termed 'the dark ages'. Possibly there was so much attention focused on the real thing that speculation about more debatable 'space' events was muted. The US government even took the chance to try to kill off UFO study once and for all, hiring sceptical scientists to write a devastating report and, in 1969, closing down its 22-year-old research programme on their recommendation. But it seriously underestimated the strength of the phenomenon, which soon came back bigger than ever.

UFO crash retrievals were not discussed during the 1960s. Indeed, most of what we know comes from retrospective studies. However, it is fascinating to see what was going on, almost undetected, as the decade unfolded and how different some of it appears from today's perspective. For ufologists now widely believe that UFO crashes can happen; indeed, they feel certain that they probably *have* happened – and often.

1961:
A SECOND SOVIET SPACEFALL

Given the enormous size of the former Soviet Union, it would seem improbable for it not to have hosted several UFO crashes, if the number being reported from the US deserts are anything to go by. Needless to say, getting information out of the Soviet authorities was very difficult and things could easily have occurred which were hushed up there more effectively than in the US. Nonetheless, aside from the Tunguska affair (discussed in Chapter one), there is another episode which has come to light, which has many chilling similarities.

On the night of 27–28 April 1961, farmers in the beautiful but rugged Karelskaya region, bordering Finland, heard a terrible roaring noise, like thunder, and then saw something remarkable illuminate the sky and then crash. Although it was not noticed at the time, witness sightings indicated a flight path strangely similar to the one reported for the 1908 object. Like the earlier one, the 1961 object first appeared to the west of Irkutsk, in Siberia. However, the 1961 object flew much further, impacting near Lake Onega, in north-western Russia.

The object was described by the farmers as being silver, metallic and cylindrical in shape. They saw it at about 2 am. Many spoke of how green smoke poured from its rear. Others likened its eventual impact to a shower of fireworks. Several told about the manner in which it 'veered crazily across the sky as it lost altitude'. In all, some 21 widely scattered farmers described seeing the object.

At 8 am the following morning, forestry-worker Vassili Brodsky was on the southern shore of Lake Onega when he came upon an incredible sight. It had not been there when he had passed the day before. Something seemed to have hit the ground, digging a huge trench, before crashing through an enormous hole in the 122-cm (4-ft) thick ice on the lake, to sink out of sight. Fearing that an aircraft may have come down, he hurried to the nearest ranger station to telephone for help from Leningrad (now St Petersburg). It was early the following morning before a team of divers and rescue experts arrived at the lake.

Victor Demidov was one of the divers. He went on to develop an interest in UFOs, not easy in the oppressive climate of the Soviet Union during the 1960s. Demidov reports that there was a huge gouge in the ground by the lake, about 27 m (88 ft) long and 15 m (50 ft) wide and between 3 and 6 m (10 and 20 ft) deep – shallowest closest to the water. The hole in the ice was round, but jagged ice blocks floated on the surface. Yet there was no sign of any cracks on the rest of the ice, although there was some free water to one side, as if the ice had melted. Whatever had caused this damage had fallen straight through the ice. In the churned-up water in the hole by the shore there were masses of tiny, grain-like pellets, black and globular in shape. Glassy and smooth to the touch, they could be ground up between the fingers.

A diver was sent into the water, but he found nothing on the bottom, except for the soil and grass gouged out of the lakeside. It had been compacted on the bottom by some huge force! Investigations with metal detectors and other equipment revealed no solid object in the lake.

The diving team decided that the object had hit the ground, dug the groove, then bounced onto the ice, landing at an acute angle and pushing the gouged-out material ahead of itself, down onto the bottom. But where was it now? Forester Brodsky was sent to the northern side of the lake to see if it could have bounced across the ice to the far shore. However, there was nothing there either. Nothing was left to explain the mystery impact.

As the investigation team took samples of the glassy balls, the fish in the lake, the chunks of ice and then collated the eyewitnesses' testimonies, the divers made one last attempt to solve the riddle. They did not find the object on the lake bed, but they discovered what had probably happened to it. On the lake bottom, beneath the hole in the ice, was a 90-m (300-ft) long, deep groove. It bent sharply and then ended suddenly. It seemed to indicate that the object had skidded along the lake bed, swerved and shot upwards, out of the water. The ice at the point where it would have exited had melted.

This would account for the disappearance of the object from the lake, but none of the eyewitnesses described seeing anything climb back into the sky after the initial impact and 'firework display'.

The blocks of ice from the site revealed another puzzle. On inspection, these gave out a curious deep emerald green cast; yet, after being removed from the water, this colour disappeared. This was noted several times but the anomaly was never resolved. The green coloration could not be reproduced by any laboratory. Everyone was baffled by the description of it offered by the witnesses at the site. Chemically, the ice did contain magnesium, aluminium, calcium, barium and titanium traces, which suggested that it had come into contact with hot metal. There were also some peculiar filament-like strands, rather like melted plastic, inside some of the snow on top of the ice.

Back in Leningrad checks were made to see if there had been any space launches, but there had been none. Even if it had been a secret mission, no spacecraft could have changed direction underwater and then taken off again – assuming that interpretation of the evidence to have been correct. There was also no trace of fire on land or rocket fuel residue, which seemed to negate this possibility.

A meteorite impact was the idea most favoured by the on-site investigators, but this was scotched in Leningrad. While it fits with the eyewitness testimony, it cannot explain the disappearance of the object or its change in direction, both in the sky or underwater. In any event, meteor expert Professor Vsevolod Sharanov of Leningrad University noted the lack of astronomical observations of any meteor at that time. There was also the shallowness of the gouge in the land, its lateral track indicating a non-vertical angle of descent and the way it shallowed out by the shore, that suggested that the object bounced off again – all of which effectively ruled out this option.

The glassy grains were found to contain silicon, iron, lithium, titanium and aluminium. They certainly resembled tektites, the globular droplets melted off from meteors at great heat and found at impact craters. However, they were unusually crumbly. Furthermore, they were almost identical to the black beads that had rained down over the Tunguska area in 1908. The official 1962 report on this residue, published in Moscow, stated that these balls were 'clearly of artificial origin'. However, their exact nature was never identified.

So what crashed into Lake Onega? Was it a strange meteor? If so, where did it disappear to afterwards and how did it behave as it did? Or was it some kind of device that fell from space, crash-landed but succeeded in taking off again? We will probably never know.

1963:
CHARLTON – THE HOLE STORY

In the summer of 1963 Beatlemania was at its height in the UK and the sunny weather drove UFOs far from people's minds. But an amazing incident occurred in leafy Wiltshire which set everyone guessing. The whole country began asking about the cause of something that literally fell from the sky and then vanished. In fact, although nobody realized it at the time, an almost identical affair had occurred at Wormer, a small village near Amsterdam, Holland, on 17 September 1959. Then, a strange whistling noise and red flash of light had been followed by the discovery of a star-shaped hole about 45 cm (18 in) in diameter in a farmer's field. The army walled off the hole and put a probe down. When it continued down after 30 m (100 ft), they gave up! Nobody could explain what had happened.

At about 6 am on 16 July, Leonard Joliffe, a dairyman at Manor Farm, Charlton, Wiltshire, claimed to hear a loud noise like a wind blast or explosion. Another local man also saw a light in the sky. A few hours later, farmhand Reg Alexander came upon a strange sight on the border between a potato field and a barley field. It was a shallow, round depression, shaped like a saucer, about 2.4 m (8 ft) wide. In the centre, there was a hole, with spokes radiating from it, each about 30 cm (1 ft) in diameter and about a metre deep. Landowner Roy Blanchard sent for the police, who quickly brought in the army and a scene almost identical to that at Wormer four years earlier was rapidly played out.

Bomb-disposal expert Captain John Rogers was soon inspecting the hole and, after finding no evidence of a bomb, stated that he could not explain what had taken place. However, the crop at the site had been totally removed and small stones were crushed to powder as if a heavy force had impacted from above. Three days after the event, the still-bemused army team got permission to probe into the hole with special equipment and reported wild readings on their detector, which indicated a large metallic object buried deep below the surface. Of course, this merely further intensified the mystery.

On 21 July the *Sunday Express* reported that new investigations were scheduled for that day, using more sophisticated equipment, 'in the hope of locating a buried metal object they

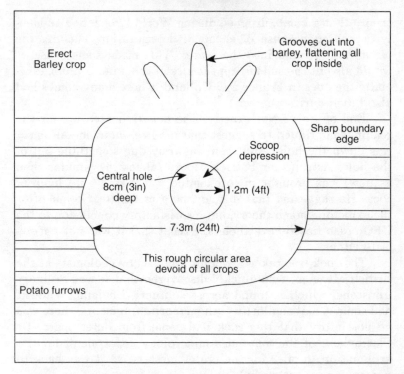

A diagram of the crater found at Charlton, Wiltshire.

have detected.' So, there clearly was something down there. However, these searches failed. On 22 July, it was reported that an army corporal, using a 'gradiometer', screeched 'It's going mad. The needle is flashing right off the end.' But dig as they might, the object, by now widely believed by UFO buffs to be a spacecraft, eluded its seekers.

About this time, the enigmatic Dr Robert Randall entered the scene. Said to have 'studied astrophysics' (*Daily Express*, 23 July), been based at the Woomera rocket test site in Australia (which he later denied, saying he merely lived there) and to have knowledge of similar holes in Australia (1954) and France (1958), he was 'convinced they were caused by a space probe craft'. Randall involved himself in the matter, at first with official blessing, which boosted his credibility no end. He caused quite a stir with TV appearances and media interviews, mooting that the UFO came from Uranus.

However, on 23 July unusual crystalline carbon deposits were dug from the hole, which completely altered the army's view of the matter. The military experts now proffered the theory that a bomb, dropped during World War 2, had suddenly detonated because of chemical deterioration, sucking the plants and ground into the crater. This made some sense; it would also fit the sudden appearance of the other craters, especially the ones in France and Holland (where many bombs had also fallen during the war).

End of story? Not exactly. The debate heated up, for the readings continued to suggest that a large, *intact* metal object was down the hole. And then the army dug something out of the hole! Astronomer Patrick Moore (almost as popular then as now) was brought in to examine a 0.25 kg (½ lb) lump of rock. He suggested that it might be a meteorite. So much for the exploding bomb theory, but a satisfactory conclusion to the UFO crash fiasco nevertheless. Except that it was not a meteorite either.

The rock was taken away for analysis by geologists at the British Museum, who quickly discovered that it was ordinary ironstone, which is found across southern England. While it had some visual similarity with meteorite fragments, there was no possibility that this rock had come from outer space. Dr Claringbell, of the museum's minerology department, had no explanation to offer for the crater mystery, so it was back to square one (or rather hole one).

Meanwhile, the Ministry of Defence (MoD) and the RAF had got in on the act and by 27 July the commander of the army unit was effectively washing his hands of the matter, confirming the incident was 'still unexplained', but claiming that, having ruled out a bomb, it was 'no part of the army's task to unravel such mysteries.'

Major Sir Patrick Wall, then a Conservative MP and member of the NATO defence committee and, much later on retirement, President of the British UFO Research Association, raised questions in Parliament about the matter. On 30 July the Secretary for War, John Godber, responded that 'no conclusive evidence' had been found to explain the cause of the impact crater but that the rock pulled out of the hole was definitely not the reason for it.

Twenty years later, when the crop circle mystery came to dominate the fields of this part of southern England, the hole in farmer Blanchard's field was dusted down by researchers for reappraisal. One witness, Graham Brunt, told Paul Fuller, editor of *The Crop Watcher*, that he had found a circle, similar to the modern ones, on the same farm back in 1951 or 1952. He confirmed this under questioning. If true, this is certainly curious.

Moreover, Wallace Binns wrote in 1992 to *The Circular*, describing time he spent on the Manor Farm field while the crater circus was under way, back in 1963. He was adamant that about 100 m (330 ft) away there was a small, flattened crop circle and that this had been seen and sketched by members of John Rogers' bomb-disposal team before the hordes of visiting sightseers, journalists and UFO buffs trampled it beyond recognition. He was sure it was just like a modern-day circle, with stalks at the edge standing erect and the crop inside pressed flat in an anti-clockwise swirl.

Some support for this story was uncovered by Paul Fuller, via a report penned by Patrick Moore. It was sent to *New Scientist* on 22 August 1963. Moore referred to an adjoining field with 'circular or elliptical areas in which the wheat had been flattened. I saw these myself . . . and [they] were certainly peculiar . . . There was evidence of "spiral flattening".' There was more to his account, but there seems little doubt from his words that the noted critic of UFO-related phenomena had personally described to a science magazine what appears to be a modern-day crop circle 17 years before that term was coined; although likely one with a mundane solution.

Two days after Moore's letter to *New Scientist*, Dr Randall was interviewed by the *Daily Sketch*. He explained why his views about a Uranian spaceship landing in that Wiltshire field had a solid basis. In fact, he had met a Uranian who emerged from a landed spaceship at Lammermuir in Scotland. Unfortunately, the doctor had tried to take off the entity's boiler suit, thus triggering a thermal device and frying the alien to a crisp. 'It was very stupid of me,' Dr Randall added. His many warnings, including those offered to then prime minister, Harold Macmillan, described the imminent alien invasion, but they were all being ignored. Dr Randall noted that his work was hampered by people making 'the most ridiculous and unlikely statements' about aliens.

The very next day, as far as the public were concerned at least, the Charlton crater affair was solved once and for all. John Southern of Wembley, London, appeared in the *News of the World* (and next day in the *Daily Mail*) and took the blame, stating he was one of three hoaxers who had dug the crater; the other two were not willing to admit their involvement. Southern said that it was part of an elaborate scheme which had been only partly carried out. The trio had planned to leave a car at the edge of the hole, with evidence that the driver had been 'snatched' by aliens. Several days later, he would appear to claim his vehicle and describe how he had been on a 'space station' in the interim.

Given that in the summer of 1963 'alien abduction' or 'spacenapping' had not been heard of, this was a devious plan, way ahead of its time. However, it is fraught with difficulties. By late August many other craters had appeared, from Southampton to Scotland; some, no doubt, just copycat hoaxes by people keen to get in on the act. But Mr Southern was unaware of most of them. Nor was he able to explain the army readings which suggested a large metal object underground.

Some days after his confession, the hoaxer wrote a detailed account for *Flying Saucer Review*, recanting. He now said that he thought the crater was a hoax. He had originally claimed responsibility for it to flush out the real culprits, since he felt sure they would never let him take the credit for their handiwork. However, nobody had come forward, so he had now concluded that the crater had to be genuine, possibly caused by a UFO.

Although attempts were made to get both the newspapers who featured the original hoax story to publish this new retraction and its reasoning, neither of them would do so, perhaps understandably fed up with it all. The *Daily Mail* effectively stated that to do this would simply leave the case open to endless speculation. This is another mystery that will probably never be resolved, unless it was a hoax after all and someone else, who was involved, eventually confesses.

1963:
UFO LANDS ON RAF BASE

One of the first cases involving a major cover-up by the British government were the events at RAF Cosford, near Wolverhampton in late 1963. These were first discussed by Les Otley of the Tyneside UFO Society in its January 1964 magazine. It was later debated by the local Press and, eventually, by *Flying Saucer Review*.

According to these sources, on about 10 December 1963 two 'RAF personnel' spotted a domed object fall to the ground behind a hangar at the RAF base. A green beam from it then swept the airfield. The witnesses ran off to get help. When they returned, they found the object had vanished. A local railway signalman reputedly also saw the object as it fell towards the base.

According to the story, a major interrogation of the witnesses took place, and then there was official silence. But what had happened to the grounded UFO? Sources referred to the unexpected appearance at the base two days after the incident of a very large aircraft. Did it ferry the UFO away?

Flying Saucer Review editor Waveny Girvan attempted to prise information first out of the base (a training school for new RAF recruits), and then the Ministry of Defence in London. The runaround he received was spectacular. Initially he was told that no incident of any kind had occurred (as was the local paper, which seemingly accepted this). Then, after Girvan had informed the authorities of data that had been privately uncovered, the official line switched to the news that there would be an investigation, followed swiftly by charges of a hoax against two 'young people' on the base. An MoD bureaucrat, B. Robson, later wrote and suggested that 'high spirits' were in evidence and that the matter was at an end.

However, BUFORA investigator Wilf Daniels was making his own enquiries in the villages surrounding the base and he heard quite a different story. By chance, he met the base's chaplain, Flight-Lieutenant Henry, who was then in the village of Albrighton adjacent to Cosford. This was before most of the UFO attention on the case began and, possibly, before the chaplain was asked by his superior officers to keep quiet. Henry was very forthcoming and had, he said, talked with the two witnesses (RAF apprentices) to help calm them: both had been very scared by what had happened. They had seen the saucer-shaped object land next to the hangar, and a door open in its side. At this point, they fled for help. Later, they were accused of being drunk, because no physical evidence of the landing had been found; but they stuck firmly to their story and the chaplain apparently believed them.

By the time Girvan arrived on the scene, Henry was incommunicado, and another base officer was dismissing the matter with a variety of solutions, including a railway signalman saying he had seen a steam engine (presumably reflected off low cloud). However, the bottom line was silence; nobody could interview Flight-Lieutenant Henry nor the two witnesses.

On 6 March, an extraordinary collection of top brass including the Secretary of State for Air, the Commander-in-Chief of the entire RAF and other assorted high-powered vice-marshalls and group commanders, arrived for what was publicly said to be an 'informal visit' of no consequence. Unsurprisingly, *FSR* magazine suspected other reasons for a visit to what was a non-operational RAF unit with fairly limited importance.

The Cosford case remains elusive. It was never really publicized and whatever happened (clearly something did, if only a misperception) was very successfully covered up. However, I can add an interesting postscript, which was offered to me in late 1988 by a man who wrote under considerable fear for his own safety. Indeed, so security conscious was he that Roy Sandbach and I had to content ourselves with meeting him at a service station on the M6 motorway for a clandestine interview 'away from prying eyes'. At no point did this man, whom I will call Don, ever mention the Cosford landing, but he was involved in an incident at the base around the same time. It was unlikely to be the same event, and seemingly occurred before it, but it does offer an insight into why the RAF was so jumpy when this UFO allegedly touched down outside one of its hangars.

Don lived at Albrighton and was a teenager at the time. He was swimming in a river beside the base with several other children. His girlfriend suddenly saw a strange object appear over the base (as if popping out of thin air). It was cigar-shaped and surrounded by an aura that caused it to glow with a curious light even in daytime. The thing was extremely close to the ground. She quickly brought it to Don's attention, but most of the other children were too far away to be attracted by them until it was too late. The object remained still for a while and then climbed in a very peculiar manner, moving sideways unlike any aircraft, rising at an astonishing rate of acceleration and vanishing. The other children were unconcerned about the matter, not having seen it very clearly, if at all. However, Don and the girl were sufficiently perturbed to go to the base and file an official report with a 'snowdrop' (as the security police there were termed). At first, the policeman was clearly sceptical, but soon saw their sincerity and took the girl's address. Don had been stealing apples from a local farm just before the incident and preferred not to be identified.

About four hours later, two RAF officers arrived at Don's

house and interrogated his parents. One identified himself as a flight-lieutenant. They had got Don's address from his girl-friend, whom they had just visited. They persuaded Don's parents to let them meet him alone in the garden, where they stayed for so long that his father became worried. However, the RAF men sent him back when he tried to come out to see what was going on. At first the officers played games with Don to test his powers of observation. Then, apparently satisfied, they implied that his girlfriend had told them a very different story. Later they admitted this was to trip him up, but Don did not change his account. Then their questions became stranger. First, they asked Don if he and his girlfriend had eaten any berries. Then, 'Did it land and leave marks?', 'Did a door open?', 'Did anyone get out?', 'Did it emit coloured smoke?' and 'Did it have a peculiar smell?'. They seemed astonishingly knowledgeable about something Don thought the British government completely rejected. Eventually, the two men told Don that the matter was a great secret and, before leaving, made his father sign a form. Over the years before he died, Don's father often reminded his son that he must never talk about the matter to anyone, hence his precautions in setting up this interview.

Attempts were made to trace his girlfriend, who had since emigrated to Australia. However, from what Don later told us, she appeared not to want to be found and was avoiding all the feelers that he put out.

1964:
ALIEN RENDEZVOUS IN NEW MEXICO

Perhaps the most persistent rumour – about which we have the least solid information – concerns an alleged alien rendezvous at Holloman, or Elmendorf, air force base in New Mexico. Even the date is arguable, spring 1964 being cited in one version. Of course, nothing may lie behind these stories. Most researchers into crashed UFO accounts in the USA have heard the tale at one time or another, but it has never been tracked down to a source. I heard it first from Dr J. Allen Hynek in about 1981, and even he had only heard it second-hand. In its basic form it describes an apparent plan to reveal the truth to the world. A (nameless) movie producer was approached by the

USAF in the early 1970s and shown amazing film footage of a UFO on the ground at a desert military base. Alien entities, seemingly alive, were also present. The film left no room for doubt about the origin of the phenomenon or the government's knowledge of it. This footage was to be used by the producer as the mainstay of an 'education programme' that would shortly bring the truth about UFOs to the world. It would be made, then left on the shelf until the time was right – seemingly not too far ahead, it was implied. However, the stunned producer never got the chance of a lifetime. He was told soon afterwards that the footage was a hoax and that he should, in fact, forget all about it.

According to some 'deep throat' sources within the US intelligence community who have befriended American ufologists since the FoI Act, there had been a battle between those who wanted to reveal the truth and those who did not, and the latter had won.

In 1980, when invited to address leading UK politicians about UFOs, I had the chance for some snatched conversations with key figures (including a former prime minister who asked not to be identified). Two separate sources told me that an 'education programme' was under slow development and that movie producers were being unconsciously involved to help reassure the public that we could survive alongside alien visitors. Of course, I have no way of knowing how true any of this was. It may have been an elaborate joke. But two years later, when Steven Spielberg's *ET*, with its cuddly alien imagery, began to entrance the world, I did remember those curious words. If there was any substance to what I was told, then Spielberg's prior interest in UFOs was simply utilized without his knowledge. Any possible barriers that might have prevented 'favourable' movies like *ET* from making their way into production were smoothed over. He (and others) were only making the movies they wanted to make. Indeed, Spielberg had a long-term fascination with UFOs (as manifested perfectly in his Oscar-winning epic *Close Encounters of the Third Kind*). In fact, Spielberg made that 1977 movie with the co-operation of Dr J. Allen Hynek (who even has a cameo role: meeting the small, egg-headed aliens at its conclusion!).

In January 1994 showbusiness columns in the USA and Britain announced that Spielberg had plans for a new spectacular UFO movie to coincide with the fiftieth anniversary of the first sightings in 1947. His focus would be UFO crash

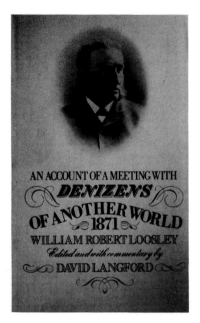

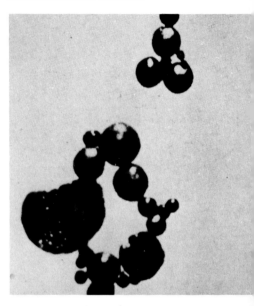

The glassy balls of solidified molten material, called tektites, found in the taiga after the Tunguska crash. Presumably, they were the result of the huge forces and tremendous heat involved.

Cover of the American edition of David Langford's book about the first claimed alien landing. There is more to this tale than meets the eye. (St Martin's Press).

The scene of devastation in the Tunguska region of Siberia, as filmed by the first expedition to reach this remote spot after the June 1908 impact by a strange object.

Right: *During World War 2 'Foo Fighters', like this one over the Pacific, were seen by Allied pilots. They were thought to be Nazi secret weapons.*

Left: *Major Jesse Marcel, looking rather embarrassed, holds some of the debris allegedly from the Roswell crash on 8 July 1947. He is at Carswell air force base in Texas and it is a matter of debate whether this material is real or not.*

Below: *One of J. Bond Johnson's famous shots taken at Carswell later that same day. Major Roger Ramey holds the press release announcing that the debris came from a weather balloon. Beside him, Colonel Thomas DuBose handles the substituted weather-balloon material. Where was the real Roswell wreckage by this time?* (J. Bond Johnson)

Left: *During the early 1950s, several photographs surfaced which allegedly showed captured aliens. This, like most, turned out be an April Fool's hoax by a German newspaper pandering to US troops.*

Below: *This supposedly depicts the alien body found in the Laredo retrieval. However, the metal frames and wiring suggest a terrestrial craft, probably an experimental US aircraft. The final proof is the spectacle frames (left of centre).*

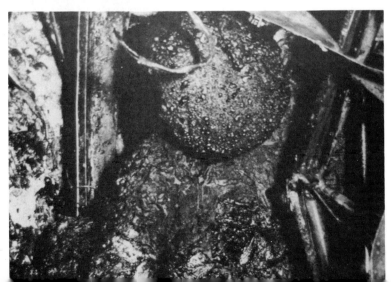

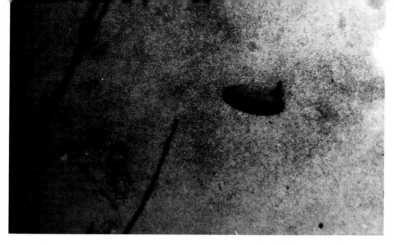

A photograph taken at Mt St Clemens, Michigan, by the Jaraslaw brothers and said by them to be a hoax. It depicts a shape remarkably like that seen at Rogue River, Ramnridge, and Fort Riley – all then unknown. (Jaraslaw)

Mufon UFO Journal

Official Publication of the Mutual UFO Network Since 1967

Number 274
February 1991
$2.50

MUFON

MUFON Journal *describes the Kecksburg, Ohio, crash of 1965.* (MUFON Journal)

Above: *Mike Sacks, who saw the UFO drop into Stacksteads quarry on 24 February 1979, stands in the Rossendale Valley and describes his encounter to ITV interviewer Fred Talbot, during filming for the children's series The Final Frontier.*

Top right: *One of the many strange lights seen over the Dalnegorsk area, on Russia's Pacific coast, where an object crashed into mountains in 1986.*

Bottom right: *A still from the video sent anonymously to American researchers, reputedly showing the object retrieved near Carp, Ontario, in 1991.*

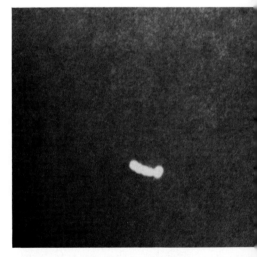

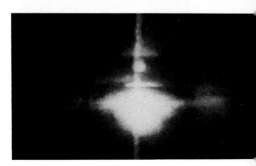

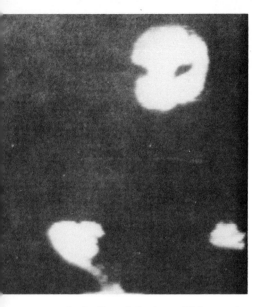

Left: *One of the few still-frame shots also supplied on the video. It supposedly shows one of the alien entities captured alive from the Ontario retrieval!*
Right: *An eyewitness from Cheshire draws the alien which entered his bedroom. This uncannily matches the descriptions from eyewitnesses and autopsy reports following half a century of retrievals.* (R. Jones)

The only flying saucer we know for certain that the USAF has flown. This experimental craft flew in the 1950s, but it was not a success. In the 1990s, stories claim the USAF flies super-secret alien craft from 'Dreamland', in the Nevada Desert.

Full transcripts of Documents 1-7, reproduced here and overleaf in their original form, appear on pages 178–84.

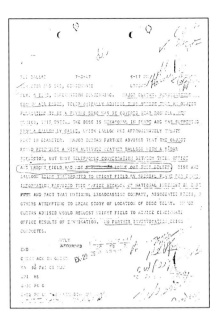

Document 1
See page 178

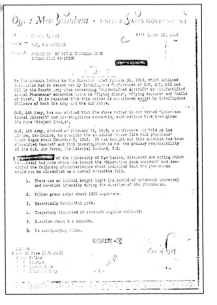

Document 2
See page 179

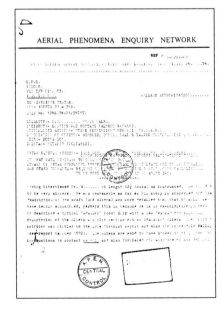

Document 3
See page 180

Document 4
See page 181

MINISTRY OF DEFENCE Defence Secretariat Division 8
Main Building Whitehall London SW1A 2HB

Telephone 01-218 (Direct Dialling)
01-218 9000 (Switchboard)

Miss J Randles
Somerville
Wallasey
Wirral

Your reference

Our reference
D/DS8/10.209

Date
13 April 1983

Dear Miss Randles,

Thank you for your recent correspondence on the subject of UFOs.

As regards your offer to summarise the reports held by this Department there really is very little to summarise. [...] I attach a copy of a blank report form showing the type of information we require together with a couple of examples of completed reports (with the name and address of the informant deleted for reasons of confidentiality). I am sure you will agree that, although we hold a large number of reports, each one is indeed very brief.

Turning now to your interest in the sighting at RAF Woodbridge in December 1980 I can confirm that USAF personnel did see unusual lights outside the boundary fence early in the morning of 27 December 1980 but no explanation for the occurrence was ever forthcoming. There is however, no question of the occurrence being a cover-up for a crashed aircraft or testing of secret devices as you suggest, nor was there any contact with "alien beings".

I understand that an article on the Woodbridge sighting has been published in the magazine "OMNI" (Vol 5 No.6) in which you may be interested.

Yours sincerely,

P J TITCHMARSH (Mrs)

Document 5
See page 182

DEPARTMENT OF THE AIR FORCE
HEADQUARTERS 81ST COMBAT SUPPORT GROUP (USAFE)
APO NEW YORK 09755

REPLY TO
ATTN OF: CD

13 Jan 81

SUBJECT: Unexplained Lights

TO: RAF/CC

1. Early in the morning of 27 Dec 80 (approximately 0300L), two USAF security police patrolmen saw unusual lights outside the back gate at RAF Woodbridge. Thinking an aircraft might have crashed or been forced down, they called for permission to go outside the gate to investigate. The on-duty flight chief responded and allowed three patrolmen to proceed on foot. The individuals reported seeing a strange glowing object in the forest. The object was described as being metallic in appearance and triangular in shape, approximately two to three meters across the base and approximately two meters high. It illuminated the entire forest with a white light. The object itself had a pulsing red light on top and a bank(s) of blue lights underneath. The object was hovering or on legs. As the patrolmen approached the object, it maneuvered through the trees and disappeared. At this time the animals on a nearby farm went into a frenzy. The object was briefly sighted approximately an hour later near the back gate.

2. The next day, three depressions 1 1/2" deep and 7" in diameter were found where the object had been sighted on the ground. The following night (29 Dec 80) the area was checked for radiation. Beta/gamma readings of 0.1 milliroentgens were recorded with peak readings in the three depressions and near the center of the triangle formed by the depressions. A nearby tree had moderate (.05-.07) readings on the side of the tree toward the depressions.

3. Later in the night a red sun-like light was seen through the trees. It moved about and pulsed. At one point it appeared to throw off glowing particles and then broke into five separate white objects and then disappeared. Immediately thereafter, three star-like objects were noticed in the sky, two objects to the north and one to the south, all of which were about 10° off the horizon. The objects moved rapidly in sharp angular movements and displayed red, green and blue lights. The objects to the north appeared to be elliptical through an 8-12 power lens. They then turned to full circles. The objects to the north remained in the sky for an hour or more. The object to the south was visible for two or three hours and beamed down a stream of light from time to time. Numerous individuals, including the undersigned, witnessed the activities in paragraphs 2 and 3.

CHARLES I. HALT, Lt Col, USAF
Deputy Base Commander

Document 6
See page 183

Document 7
See page 184

retrievals and the US government. Moreover, there was a further story about top-secret film footage of UFOs on the ground at some military site which, as the story indicated, may have found its way to Spielberg's production company and stimulated interest. There was no confirmation or denial, but Spielberg's continued interest in UFOs appears genuine enough.

In addition, in March 1994 I was told of the embryonic plans of another top movie producer who was intrigued by a case about a UFO crash-landing at a military base in England, which, in fact, occurred only a few days after the extraordinary day that I had spent in Westminster in December 1980. Is some clever plan afoot, using unwitting sources to assist it?

Robert Emenegger, a film producer, contributed a chapter titled 'On being contacted', to a book in 1974 which was published to coincide with the release of his film *UFOs: Past, Present and Future*. In the book, Emenegger describes an episode at Holloman base. This base is within that sensitive triangle of desert land where, during the 1940s and 1950s, UFO crashes seem to have been a regular occurrence. It is also where secret aircraft and rocket technology were being developed. According to Emenegger, he was presenting 'an incident that might happen in the future – or perhaps could have happened already.' His 'Holloman scenario', as he termed it, was about a UFO landing at Holloman, where it was apparently expected by some high-ranking government officials. Senior air force personnel communicated, in a non-verbal way, with living alien entities who emerged from their craft. The whole episode was filmed for posterity. It would be the retrieval to end all retrievals – the ultimate proof of UFO reality, in fact.

Emenegger did something interesting with this 'story'. He showed it to various leading sociologists and psychologists and asked them to suggest what would be the impact if that film actually existed and were screened to the world. There was a big difference of opinion. Some concluded that those unwilling to believe would still not believe, however strong the proof within the film: they would suspect a government hoax was involved.

In 1990, while writing *Looking for the Aliens*, I asked Emenegger for his opinions on the strength of evidence for alien contact. He replied that he rejected the contactee tales from the 1950s, considered modern accounts of abduction and spacenapping as the products of something 'within the mind' and yet still, apparently, felt that ET visitation was 'not only possible, but very probable, judging from the evidence I have seen.' He then added, rather intriguingly, that 'from my information it [an alien landing] has happened in May of 1971 ... other reports put it also on 30 December 1980 in England, both at military bases'. The latter is clearly the alleged encounter at Woodbridge air force base in Suffolk, referred to earlier and discussed in some detail later (see pages 131–148). The former, I can only assume, are the legendary events at the Holloman/ Elmendorf base in New Mexico. Indeed, it is fascinating that one of the first witnesses who spoke off the record in 1983 about his association with the Woodbridge landings said that he recalled meeting another stunned airman at the landing site. That man was repeating in shock, 'not again, not again'. It later emerged that he had been present at a similar episode – at Elmendorf air force base several years earlier.

1964:
TRILOGY – ANOTHER AIR BASE RETRIEVAL

Given the episodes at Cosford in England and in New Mexico in late 1963 and early 1964, the existence of a third claim about an air-base UFO landing is certainly remarkable. It seems to form a bizarre pattern and partially overcomes the fact that the case which now completes the trilogy is based upon only two eyewitness accounts. David gave his testimony to Len Stringfield in 1978. He was on guard duty at the motor pool at Fort Riley army base in Kansas. The date was 10 December 1964; the time, 2 am (most intriguingly, exactly a year, virtually to the minute, after the Cosford encounter). He and three other men were rounded up by a senior officer and issued with extra ammunition. Then, they were despatched to a remote corner of the base, where they had to walk the last kilometre to reach the designated spot. As they arrived, a large helicopter with a searchlight was illuminating a strange object on the ground. Various other army personnel were already in attendance, including a major-general. He ordered David to patrol around the craft and shoot anyone who tried to get near it. David was also sternly advised what would happen if he ever spoke about what he was witnessing. For two and a half hours David did his duty, with the helicopter periodically searching adjacent fields, as if looking for more debris. He was then relieved and sent back to base just before dawn.

The object was described as like a giant hamburger, some 12 m (40 ft) across and 4.5 m (15 ft) high, with a dark line along its rim and a very small tail-fin stabilizer: a most unusual design. There was no sign of a door or any life within it, but David said that whenever he was close to it, the air felt warm, although it was a very cold night. David discussed this matter reluctantly and under strict secrecy, but he did later establish his credentials, proving that he was on the base at the time of the incident and showing a letter, clearly sent at the time indicated. This was dated 11 December 1964 and went to his fiancée in another state. In the letter, he referred to 'special duty' that was 'in the boondocks of Ft Riley' at which he had guarded 'some odd thing in a field . . . probably some new type of aircraft'. After going public with his story, David was contacted (indirectly) by a man who had been reminded of an incident that had happened at about 7 am on that same morning. He had not really given it a second thought before then.

This man, who eventually contacted Len Stringfield to confirm the matter but was clearly reluctant to get involved, had driven out to the same part of the base while waiting for a breakfast-time duty to start. He had come upon a restricted access sign but no guards, so he went around it, until he met some men with guns and was ordered out in no uncertain terms. However, before he left, he noticed a large, flat-bed truck with a roundish object on top, completely covered in canvas so that its precise nature was not visible. Half a dozen men, wearing white suits and face masks (like germ-warfare-protection suits), were standing beside the truck.

If this report is sincere, it offers clear support for David's story and strong evidence that some kind of device was retrieved from this location, but that does not establish its extraterrestrial nature, of course. The possibility that it was something like the AV Roe circular saucer craft, designed for army use in 1960, cannot be ruled out. This possibility takes a serious knock, though, when it is discovered that what is a virtual clone of this object has been seen by various completely unrelated witnesses over a very long period of time; so long that it simply cannot have been a secret aircraft under test, not for that many years and in so many diverse locations.

I first came across this shape in an account given to me by witness Bill Dillon of Luton, in the UK, who saw the object

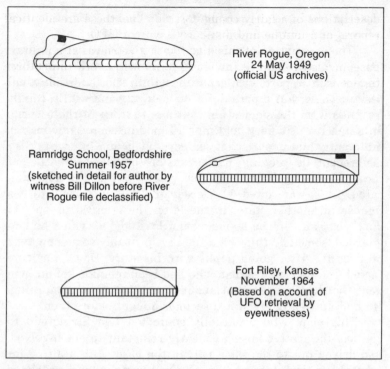

River Rogue, Oregon
24 May 1949
(official US archives)

Ramridge School, Bedfordshire
Summer 1957
(sketched in detail for author by
witness Bill Dillon before River
Rogue file declassified)

Fort Riley, Kansas
November 1964
(Based on account of
UFO retrieval by
eyewitnesses)

A comparison between the UFO seen at Rogue River, Rambridge, and Fort Riley.

flying over Ramridge School one lunchtime in May 1957. His very detailed description and sketches reached me before David's story appeared. However, once the Fort Riley case was published, the comparisons were obvious. Even before Dillon's information, I had received a copy of a USAF investigation file released under the FoI Act in 1978. This third case included a detailed account and drawing of an object seen by fishermen at Rogue River, Oregon, in May 1949. The description of the shape, performance and various subtle features of the craft itself leave very little room for doubt that it is precisely the same device being witnessed three times over a period of 15 years. There are even some contentious photographs, taken in Michigan in January 1967, which may show this particularly unusual type of craft.

If this were a police investigation seeking witness accounts of a very distinctive vehicle, then these cases would probably constitute sufficient proof of multiple observations. We are not simply talking about a series of vaguely similar descriptions of a fairly common stereotype, these are identical reports of a unique and distinctive type of UFO.

The association of this affair with a retrieval at a military base in also certainly intriguing. But why were there three independent reports of a grounded object spotted inside a military base within a period of precisely 12 months? Especially, coupled with the suggestion that at least one of these events might have involved friendly communication between the authorities and aliens, rather like that climactic scene in *Close Encounters of the Third Kind*.

1965:
THE FIRST PHOTOGRAPH

A mini-sensation occurred in UFO circles early in 1965 when, for the first time, a crashed UFO was reputedly photographed from the air. What is more this picture defied secrecy to reach ufologists.

According to the South American Press, the incident occurred in early January 1965 at San Miguel, in the foothills of the Andes, near Mendoza, Argentina. Various anonymous local ranchers apparently described how they had seen the UFO come down and spotted small creatures moving around outside it. These beings wore divers' suits and emitted a green phosphorescence. This was not an auspicious start!

However, according to the media reports, a local aviation authority Cessna aircraft was sent to the location, which is fairly remote and rugged. A glow from the object easily attracted the aircrew to it and they were able to capture the first, close-up, aerial views of the device as they swooped overhead. It was cigar-shaped or tubular and about 8 m (25 ft) long and 1 m (3 ft) wide. Speculation about its origin had settled on it being some kind of debris from a space mission that had fallen back to earth, even though it appeared relatively intact.

The local newspapers did not feature any of these priceless pictures, alleging that the Mendoza police chief had issued a special order to prevent them from doing so. Meanwhile, the Argentine Air Force reputedly arrived and shipped the device to the national space centre at Córdoba. Here it was found to be only half the size estimated from the air. At first glance, it resembled an aircraft engine. However, according to the stories, its sides were pitted with evidence of high impact damage, suggesting entry into the atmosphere. Furthermore, the metal from which it was made could not be identified. Argentine ufologist Oscar Galindez was eventually able to get hold of a copy of a copy of one photograph. Despite its poor quality, it showed an object resting on the sandy scrubland and casting a deep shadow, more or less as described by the stories.

However, ufologists have since entertained some serious doubts about this case. The South American Press were notorious during the 1960s for trying to outdo one another with remarkable stories. None of the sources involved appears to have ever confirmed that this event happened and none of the nameless ranchers came forward to support the account. As for the photograph, proper analysis is not possible on a copy of a copy, but there are worries even with what is available. The object appears to analysts to be much smaller than alleged – perhaps only a few inches long, although certainty is impossible. If it were really so small, then, far from being a large fallen object photographed from the air, it would probably be a model on a table-top, photographed at close quarters. Indeed, this photograph has some similarity with a 1950s shot reputedly showing a landed UFO and its spacesuit-clad occupant standing alongside it. This reportedly came from the Italian Alps, but it is widely accepted as being a small, hand-made model taken from only a few feet away.

We may never have assurance about the San Miguel retrieval case, without any witnesses to tell their story firsthand or negatives to properly assess the image. Even if it is genuine, then without these attributes it cannot be taken seriously. It has to be said that few ufologists think this remarkable case likely to contribute to our knowledge. The first (and for many years the only) photograph of an alleged UFO retrieval sitting on the ground is thus a considerable disappointment.

1965:
THE GREAT LAKES BOLIDE

At about 4.45 pm on 9 December 1965, hundreds of witnesses in southern Canada, Michigan, Ohio and Pennsylvania observed a UFO crash down from the sky. From the many descriptions of a fiery mass spewing smoke trails, there seems, at first, to be little doubt that it was a bright fireball meteor. But this was to be a most peculiar meteor which, 30 years later, is still hotly debated by the various experts. Indeed, for many this case is another Roswell – uncontestable evidence of an alien retrieval.

There is no question that something happened that afternoon; far too many independent witnesses spotted the object and it was immediately reported in the newspapers. The theory of a bright meteor was quickly proposed, with so much assurance that the stories soon faded. Then, in March 1966, scientist and UFO researcher Ivan Sanderson compiled an account from the various eyewitness stories and first noted the problems with this conclusion.

It was possible to look at the sightings in some detail and recognize a number of things. The object showed a clear trajectory, moving from the north-west to the south-east. In all, its passage took at least six minutes, which indicates a speed far too slow for a meteor that would be burning up high in the atmosphere and pass by in seconds. Sanderson calculated a speed of only 1,600 km/hr (1,000 mph), which, if accurate, would rule out a meteor (or bolide as these are technically termed). But this slow speed should have provided a far longer spread of timings, given the 800-km- (500-mile-) plus path traced by the UFO, so it is probably an underestimate.

Sightings not only involved witnesses on the ground – reporting the orange flare, the smoke trail and pieces falling off the object – but several pilots spoke of being buffeted by shock waves as the thing passed them. This is unique, because in all previous bolide cases the object was high in the atmosphere, far above aircraft. There were also stories of a sonic boom (for example, at Port Clinton in Ohio) and vibrations felt on the ground akin to an earthquake (at Acme, Pennyslvania). The smoke trail was so intense that it remained visible for up to 20 minutes and was filmed by a witness at Pontiac, Michigan. At Lapeer, Michigan, bits of silvery debris were found on the ground and assumed to have fallen from the passing object. However, later analysis by the US Air Force conclusively showed them to be chaff – pieces of aluminium foil released by aircraft during aerial exercises to fool radar screens with the production of multiple reflections.

Another of the reasons why Sanderson disputed the hastily drawn official conclusion that the object was a bolide is that during the final few miles of the sighting trail, the object

103

clearly appeared to turn easterly. A course change by a descending bolide is impossible, but it was, if you recall, just what was observed to occur at Tunguska in 1908.

There are no reports of the object south of Pennsylvania because several people in Kecksburg, near Mount Pleasant, some 30 km (20 miles) south-east of Pittsburgh, saw and heard it crash into a wooded area near by. Two children playing in the woods reported a 'star on fire' that fell from the sky and exploded. They persuaded their mother to call the state police, who not surprisingly interpreted it (and other reports received) as an aircrash. They immediately set off for the forest, after calling out the fire service. However, they were nearly beaten to the site by a military unit, which took command and apparently knew everything about the crash. The police and fire service were soon told to leave the woods. A few hours later, the military team told them that they had found nothing. They concluded that the object was a meteor, so everyone could go to bed and forget about it. At 2 am the military left the area.

For many years that was how the story remained: an innocuous bolide that had provoked what proved to be spurious reports of having crashed at Kecksburg, interesting merely for the way in which it showed the rapidity of military response to any event which even had a hint of being an unknown object that was potentially retrievable.

UFO researchers, like everybody else, forgot all about the case. But events were to prove them very wrong for doing so. Fortunately, unlike at Roswell, it was not to be another 30 years before the importance of the affair became recognized. By the time the truth was sought, there was still opportunity to track down many of those who were directly involved.

In January 1980 UFO investigator Clark McClelland spoke with the assistant fire chief of Kecksburg (James Mayes) and another member of his team (Melvin Reese). What they had to say was very interesting. The fire team had come within 60 m (200 ft) of the object before being turned away by the military unit. They had spotted blue flashing lights, but there was no fire in the woods. However, something was on the ground, having smashed its way through trees and embedded itself there. Mayes explained how the military cordoned off the woods and set up a temporary base at the fire station, with telecommunications directly linking them to higher authorities. This seems difficult to equate with a search for a piece of meteor, as the firemen were later informed. Mayes also saw a flat-bed truck leave the wood some hours later, carrying an object covered by cloth. Eventually, the fire chief himself (Robert Bitner) was traced. He said that he had seen the thing clearly. It was about 1.8 m (6 ft) high, 2 m (7 ft) wide and some 5 m (17 ft) long, resting at an angle on the ground as if it had come in near horizontally – not vertically. He saw it from about 8 m (25 ft) before being ushered away by military guards.

These reports certainly made the case look much more interesting and Stan Gordon, a respected paranormal researcher from Pennsylvania, took up the cause. In 1987 he spoke with 'Pete', one of the other fire officers on site, who confirmed that the team thought they were dealing with a plane crash until they got there and saw the object and noted the military's intense interest in it. He described it as a 'large acorn-shaped object embedded deep into the ground', adding that it seemed to have come in at a 30-degree angle, knocking off tree tops and flattening one tree near the point of contact; but it was remarkably intact. Lying on its side, you could see its base, where there was a set of rings or bumpers into which were inscribed some pictorial symbols 'like hieroglyphics'.

Yet again, we hear this remarkable reference to the same type of peculiar picture writing found in other crashes since the Victorian era – although it should be noted that when Pete told his story in 1987, the Roswell case was public knowledge. However, he made no reference to Roswell in his testimony.

Because there was now some speculation about the object being a Russian spacecraft, Pete was asked about the hiero-glyphics; being of Polish descent, he could read Russian. He was adamant that they were not Russian. Furthermore, Pete shocked the investigators by saying: 'I'll stake my life on it; the object was not man-made.'

As Stan Gordon's investigation proceeded, Ray Boeche used the FoI Act to appeal for official documents about the recovery. This proved difficult but, in 1985, 30 pages of data were procured. The information was fairly low key, comprising mostly letters making enquiries and a few eyewitness reports of the light passing through the sky, but there was one very interesting note: a memo submitted by a USAF investigator with Project Blue Book and sent to his head at Wright Patterson air force base in Dayton, Ohio. This spoke of how 'a three-man team has been dispatched to [Kecksburg] to investi-gate and pick up an object that started a fire.' In other words, this was written confirmation that, even before they got to the site, something was known to the authorities to have crashed and be retrievable. The conclusion to the report flatly denies this idea. There were certainly errors in the released file. This reference to a fire is borne out by no other known testimony or evidence. The file also gives the time of the incident as 4.15 pm, despite carrying letters which give the correct times. The final conclusion of the file was that the UFO was a meteor, that nothing was recovered and that, after making checks, 'there was no space debris which entered the atmosphere on 9 December 1965'. This seemed to rule out the other most popular theory: that the device was some kind of space vehicle. Certainly the bell, conical or acorn shape (terms used by various witnesses) is not unlike a space capsule in design or reported size. The military unit involved in the attempted retrieval was identified by the file as the Oakdale Radar Unit, based near Pittsburgh airport. Later enquiries revealed it to be from Aerospace Defence Command, with special training for space missions. It is known to have set up a direct link with NORAD from the fire station that night (NORAD being the radar set up to record and track any intrusion from orbit, including enemy satellite and space flight movements, as well as intercontinental ballistic missiles).

For a time, this provided a clue. A Russian military satellite (Cosmos 96) was known to have been brought back to earth on or around 9 December. The speculation was that the Americans might have recovered it, perhaps even the nuclear reactor that could have driven the craft. If true, this would explain the secrecy surrounding the affair and the need to recover and then drive the object away to the security of an air base as fast as possible.

The main problem with this theory is that the debris should have burnt up on its re-entry into the atmosphere. Today debris from satellites is regularly raining down on the earth, now that thousands of them are in temporary orbit. While small pieces of wreckage do occasionally get through (for example, a radioactive component from a Russian satellite fell on Canada in late 1977), a huge intact satellite seems most unlikely to beat the inferno-like heat and terrible stresses of re-entry through the atmosphere.

Eventually, after much stalling by other authorities, NASA released data on Cosmos 96. It had indeed re-entered on 9 December, but at 3.15 am (Pennsylvania time). This was 13 hours too early for the UFO events and so seemingly rules out this spacecraft as a solution to the Kecksburg affair.

Stan Gordon's research in and around Kecksburg in the late 1980s traced another witness, Jack, who was able to describe first-hand the events of that night. He had been in his car near his home close by the impact point when he saw some lights in the wood. He drove up a little track (now called Meteor Road because that night it was choked with cars from the investigating police, fire service and military chasing the 'meteor'). Jack saw a group of people surrounding an object like a large bullet embedded in the ground. He used his car headlights to illuminate the spot. Some blue sparks were coming off the surface of the unusual metal. These continued for several minutes before dying down.

In September 1990 the US TV series *Unsolved Mysteries* reported the case. Afterwards, two new witnesses came forward with stories that seemed to make some sense, in the light of what was known. One man was a USAF officer at Lockbourne air force base, near Columbus, Ohio (about 250 km/150 miles west of the site). In the early hours of 10 December, a truck arrived by the little-used back gate and he was one of the guards set to patrol around it for several hours. It was a flat-bed with a large tarpaulin on the surface covering some kind of conical object. He was told to shoot anyone who tried to get too close! He was relieved at 7 am and, 30 minutes later, the truck was driven away. He was advised that it was bound for Wright Patterson.

Wright Patterson air force base, the reputed home of the other crashed UFOs, is the obvious choice for the destination of this recovered object, whatever it was. Housing the Foreign Technology Division (or FTD), the base had the facilities to analyse the device. It was also, by chance, only 300 km (200 miles) from Kecksburg. Lockbourne lies directly between the site and Wright Patterson and seems a logical secure stopping-off point.

The other witness was a building contractor who said that two days later, on 12 December 1965, he was asked to take a load of 6,500 special bricks to a hangar inside Wright Patterson. This was well guarded, but he sneaked a look inside before being thrown out by armed security men. There was a bell-shaped device, some 4 m (14 ft) high, sitting there, with its top covered by a parachute-like canopy that was partly raised. Several men wearing white 'radiation'-style suits and gas masks were inspecting the object. This sounds very similar to the story from the officer who saw identically clad men working beside the craft at Fort Riley, Kansas, the year before. Then, after being escorted out of the hangar, a guard told the witness that he had just seen an object which would become common knowledge 'in 20 years time'. Of course, sadly, that appears not to be the case.

1967:
SUMMER MADNESS

The warning signs were there two years earlier, but they did not prevent one of the greatest mysteries of all time from taking hold. On 13 September 1965, police in south London got a most unusual call from power-station workers to go to the River Thames near the Dartford Tunnel. The reason? A flying (or rather *floating* saucer) was visible in the muddy water, too far out to reach from the shore. On arrival, the police officers were shocked to learn that this was no crank call. There really was a large, conical object in the water. So they set up a patrol and searched the area, finding only some youths 'ship spotting' up a tree.

Eventually the object was recovered. It was a large, aluminium cone with a wooden frame, some 1.8 m (6 ft) high, which looked like a miniature space capsule. The letters HOR 25-2 were written on it. After carefully opening it, the police found rubber inner tubes to keep it afloat and a note asking it to be returned to students at the Royal Aircraft Technical College at Farnborough. (Ironically, Farnborough is the place where the secret study of UFOs was set up in the mid-1950s according to various RAF sources, so it is the British equivalent of Wright Patterson air force base.) Later, Peter Mucci, chairman of the student rag committee (one of the people up the tree!), came forward to explain that it was a stunt to promote their fundraising. He and five other students had ferried the cone to the river on a truck in the middle of the night, and then watched to see what happened. The letter H stood for Herbert, their pet name for the UFO, OR were the letters on cars in the Farnborough area and 25-2 symbolized their coming rag week – 25 September to 2 October.

Stunts like this are always to be expected, but this played on the interest in NASA space missions at the time, as well as in the UFO mystery. The cone would have cost about £100 to build today. It was constructed in a garage. Fortunately, the police saw the funny side and the students, of course, got all the rag publicity they wanted.

Two years later, UFOs hit Britain in a big way. The wave really struck during October 1967, provoking major debates in Parliament, but there was a gradual escalation of sightings in the weeks beforehand. These were fuelled by another remarkable discovery that was so bizarre it seemed unlikely to be a hoax.

Just after dawn on 4 September 1967, a paperboy at Clevedon, near Bristol, found a strange object in a field. It was a classic flying saucer in every sense: disc-like, about 1.5 m (5 ft) wide, grey and immobile. It was recovered by the police and handed over to the chief design engineer at the guided weapons division of British Aerospace, who admitted to being baffled. He estimated that if it were a hoax, it was an expensive one: today the disc would cost £350 to make. Soon it became apparent that there was far more to this story than one little saucer: five more identical objects were also discovered across southern England!

The devices were on golf courses or in farmers' fields. Athough it was some time before the facts were co-ordinated, they had, it seemed, landed on a 350-km (220-mile) long straight line, exactly spanning one line of latitude. They ran from Clevedon in the west, more or less equally spaced, to the Isle of Sheppey in the Thames estuary, Kent. At each location, the response was different. At Chippenham, in Wiltshire, the bomb-disposal team which had gone to the Charlton crater (see page 88) was called out. After prodding the saucer for a while, they took it to the local rubbish dump and blew it up. This revealed a good deal about the true nature of the spaceship, but it was a rather pre-emptive thing to do.

At Welford, the USAF became very intrigued and an intelligence officer took photographs, no doubt for despatch to Project Blue Book back in the USA. Home Office chemists also cautiously took samples of a liquid that seeped out, smelling like rotten eggs. They took it to the chemical warfare site at Aldermaston for an in-depth study.

The RAF sent a helicopter to the Isle of Sheppey and immediately cordoned off the site before airlifting the device to their base at Manston in Kent.

However, there was no mass panic, unlike the fears

expressed by the doom merchants who claim that proof of alien contact would send people screaming into the streets. Rather, this affair sent folk scouring the countryside looking for more spacecraft, even though for the first few hours the matter was taken very seriously because it seemed as if aliens really had landed in southern England. At Bromley, in Kent, the UFO was taken by the police to the lost property office at the railway station, where it was examined by a Ministry of Defence expert. This one, like several of the craft, emitted a curious 'bleeping' sound which, upon opening, was found to come from a home-made speaker and transmitter powered by batteries.

Gradually, of course, the truth did sink home. The objects had all been moulded out of a type of fibreglass and were fairly light. The smelly liquid was a concoction of flour and water. Each saucer had cost far less to make than the estimate by the guided weapons expert (perhaps £500 in all at today's prices) and had been transported by car in a co-ordinated exercise involving about 15 people. It was, if you had not already guessed, another rag stunt masterminded by two of the same students at the college in Farnborough who had been part of the Thames prank in 1965. However, on this occasion there was a far higher price to pay for their fundraising. While they do not seem to have been charged with anything, there was a mammoth bill for the taxpayer as a result of police, scientific and military activity during that day. Mission controller Chris Southall admitted that he was convinced that 'flying saucers will land on earth some day' and that this exercise was partly designed 'to give the police and experts a bit of practice'.

There are interesting lessons to be learnt from the farrago. Although it was very quickly established that this was just a joke – typical of the British sense of humour that spawned the Monty Python comedy team around this same time – it might not have been. The reaction displayed is unlikely to have been much different if these had been real spacecraft and one wonders how any cover-up could have coped with such a multiple landing.

Had this happened in the USA, it would have been the 'nightmare scenario' for the USAF, where no end of rapid response could have probably succeeded in keeping the lid on what had really happened. The way in which this story appeared in the media across the UK within minutes of the first discovery must pose serious questions about the viability of the alleged cover-up. Hiding retrieved spacecraft in the USA time after time and year after year seems hard to fit into what took place on this occasion. Also, given that a group of dedicated people with the will and the ability were so readily able to create such a masterful hoax for pure fun, it should make all researchers beware of insisting that a case cannot possibly be a hoax because it is too complex or lacks obvious motivation. In Britain, certainly, any major UFO event during the early autumn needs to be watched with more than one eye on the student fraternity!

CHAPTER SIX

THE LEAN YEARS

The 1970s were, for some reason, strangely devoid of reports of UFO crashes. Indeed only two, rather tenuously linked, if fascinating, stories survive. There could be a number of reasons for this. Perhaps, the UFOs just were not crashing any more. Or, then again, the authorities may have improved their techniques for hiding the evidence. Another factor was the abandonment of official UFO study by the USAF in 1969, which defused public interest until later in the decade. Whatever the case, this decade certainly qualifies for the description: 'the lean years'.

However, it is worth noting that there was another distraction: the rise of alien abduction and spacenapping stories. Perhaps this turned researchers away from the search for data about crash retrievals and on to the latest fad that seemed to offer a chance of a breakthrough. Remember that for most of the decade retrieval was still a dirty word and nobody was really taking UFO crashes seriously – not even the ufologists! In any event, the lull was short-lived. By 1978 the FoI Act had allowed documents to be squeezed out of the US government, opening cases from the past. Soon Len Stringfield and others were vigorously delving into the records in search of witnesses to the great cover-up. This was swiftly followed in 1980 by publication of *The Roswell Incident* by William Moore and Charles Berlitz, after which the hunt for crashed UFO stories was really on.

1974:
THE NIGHT THE MOUNTAIN EXPLODED

In the mid- to late 1970s my boyfriend's family had a caravan at Llandrillo, a tiny village beside the River Dee midway between Corwen and Bala Lake in Clwyd, North Wales. It is a beautiful spot. We loved it because it was so quiet. We could ride there from Chester on his Triumph motorcycle and spend day after day walking in the Berwyn Mountains or relaxing by the river. I did some of the work on my first three UFO books out there.

Once, I remember visiting a little pub in the village and hearing about the night the mountain exploded. This intrigued me and, even though the locals were not all that forthcoming, particularly with 'foreigners' from England, one elderly chap did talk about it since we were semi-regular visitors to the area.

The event had occurred on a cold night in the winter of 1974. There had been a terrible bang. The entire village had heard it and thought something had exploded. Going outside, people saw blue and orange lights floating in a circle around Cader Bronwen, the mountain that rises to the east of the village. The old man also told me there was a peculiar buzzing noise in the air for a few minutes, like a swarm of bees. I asked if he had gone to see what was happening before the lights disappeared, but he said no. They were told later in the night that a plane had crashed and the authorities had it under control. I did not recall a plane crash in the area, but I was familiar with the low-flying RAF jets that screamed over our campsite and hugged the valley contours. They came, I understand, from RAF Shawbury in Shropshire. Perhaps one of these had had an accident.

Then the old man told me that it had not been an air crash. They had just been told that at the time to keep them off the mountain. What did he mean, I enquired, by now intrigued. He smiled and said, 'Nobody knew for sure. They just told us they thought it was a meteor, but found nothing.' These words jogged my memory about a story that briefly made the news several years previously. I had never connected it with Llandrillo, knowing only that something had happened in North Wales.

I did a bit of digging after that, but nobody in the area would talk to me. To be honest, I never really took the case seriously then, when I was still visiting Llandrillo regularly, and I have been angry with myself ever since for being hoodwinked like everybody else. Everything that is surfacing about this affair suggests that it was another Kecksburg (see page 104), and there is increasing evidence that this may be the best example of a UFO retrieval in Britain.

There were many local, and several national, Press reports

113

in the immediate wake of the incident. It even made the TV news the night it occurred (23 January 1974), and the national Press the next morning. What follows is a summary of various reports, including some first-hand research by Tony Pace (an astronomer with BUFORA) and Eileen Buckle, then a secretary at *FSR* magazine. At the time, everyone seemed to think that it was a fireball meteor, or bolide; as such, no work was ever taken beyond basic data collection.

There was a huge explosion a few minutes after 8.30 pm. From various accounts, this preceded (some say by up to two or three minutes) a violent shaking of the ground, like a medium-sized earthquake – objects inside houses were knocked off shelves. Only a small area was affected; it does not seem to have been widespread. Earthquakes in North Wales are quite common: I have experienced two myself, including one that toppled a painting off my wall in Stockport, about 80 km (50 miles) from its epicentre. The unstable Bala Fault runs through North Wales. All the earthquakes are feeble, but the inhabitants certainly know about them.

If the explosion occurred before the tremor, as by all accounts it did, then that is interesting. It suggests that the former was a sonic boom or shock wave from a high-speed flying object that hit the mountain, causing the earth tremor. The object, of course, could have been a spaceship, aircraft or a meteorite.

Hard evidence for the earth tremor was obtained via the seismological unit at Edinburgh University. It actually recorded it, at 8.39 pm. It immediately assumed that it was a mundane earthquake and, by virtue of being able to measure it some 400 km (250 miles) away, it could estimate that it had been quite strong and pinpoint its focal point as the Bala area.

The reports of lights in the sky are confused by the fact that at 9.58 pm a very bright fireball meteor (at least that is what the astronomers think it was) did pass across the skies of Britain from the east, over North Wales, where many people witnessed it, still being outside after the explosion and ground tremors. In later reports, all three events tended to get compressed together, and the fireball was often wrongly assumed to have coincided with the other two events. The coastguard at Holyhead, on Anglesey, for instance, spotted the object and described it as like a giant tadpole spouting flames, which certainly fits the meteor diagnosis. Alternatively, the old spectre of satellite debris re-entering the atmosphere might have been raised by this incident, but no re-entry was due that night.

The lights on the mountain were different, but tended to get relegated in importance behind the more spectacular thing in the sky. This is a shame, because they clearly were connected with whatever struck the mountain. Tony Pace (very perceptively) did see the distinction between the two light phenomena, concluding they were unrelated and suggested as early as September 1974 that the glow over Cader Bronwen was 'that poorly understood electrical phenomenon associated with earth movement – those strange earthquake lights'.

Eileen Buckle was more open to the UFO theory, and associated a number of UFO sightings over a three-day period around the explosion to bolster this, including one in Durham, 240 km (150 miles) north-east of Bala. In the end she could only contend that nobody knew what had happened.

Certainly, the most curious feature of the story was the Press reports on 24 January (subsequently supported by what the man in the pub told me) that the authorities responded very rapidly. Police received 999 calls reporting an 'air crash' (origin of the first story circulating around the village), but on checking with the RAF (it seems from RAF Valley on Anglesey) they soon learnt of the lights in the sky and meteor theory. However, they responded in a remarkable way. They cordoned off the mountainside and sent up a team of police, followed by RAF experts with a helicopter. Then nobody was allowed into the area, not even police. Given that this is one of the bleakest uninhabited regions in the UK, these seem extreme precautions. And the restrictions remained in force for several days.

The media never really followed up this aspect. The RAF told us that it was searching for debris from a meteor fall. A few days later it called off the search, saying it had found nothing. End of story. But in retrospect it does seem bizarre that the RAF would go to so much trouble to protect an area where so very few people were likely to venture anyway. Nor would we expect it to spend a lot of time and money looking for a bit of rock. No – this reaction seems too great for its alleged cause and implies something rather more than a supposed meteor on the mountain. It suggests something that the RAF – as opposed to the police or mountain rescue team, who were soon sent home – had a paramount interest in securing.

In 1981 Paul Devereux remembered the case while compiling his epic volume *Earthlights*, in which he assesses the theory that many UFOs are a product of earthly energies trig-gered from rocky fault-lines. Understandably, he saw this case as a good example of his theory. Devereux notes that the lights seen by locals were centred on Arthur's Table, a small hill on the Llandrillo side of Cader Bronwen. An interesting stone cir-cle is situated on the bleak moors here. This suits his hypoth-esis well, because he sees a relationship between these old sites and the energies trapped in the rocks at certain locations. Perhaps the ancients deified places where these visual displays occasionally happened, building ceremonial circles there. One of Devereux's researchers found that there had been a pletho-ra of fireball activity during that January night in 1974. He cites a white light over the Isle of Man and multiple balls of light in the sky above the Bristol Channel. Nearer to Bala, people referred to 'red disc-like lights encircling the mountain'. However, of most importance was his discovery, via Keith Critchlow, that a few days after the incident – with the RAF off the mountain – two scientists had visited the stone circle for a routine check. They found unusually high radiation read-ings in the area. As a result of this unexpected outcome, Devereux's research team later took Geiger-counter readings at other circle sites to see what they might reveal about these puzzling earth energies.

So, we have clear evidence of a localized impact on the mountain, strange glowing lights immediately in its wake, a rapid RAF response, extreme reaction and persistence in its still-unexplained search operation and subsequent evidence within the week that radiation readings in the area were unusually high. This is certainly a strong *prima facie* case for something having crashed up there. Of course, one might be tempted to think that an aircraft had crashed there while car-rying a nuclear weapon. This would certainly have justified a major RAF clear-up operation.

In 1985 I was invited with Peter Hough to speak to the offi-cers' club at RAF Shawbury. Many attentive senior airmen were present, one of whom told us he had flown in from RAF Valley by private jet just to listen to us. Afterwards, everyone was very co-operative and swapped anecdotes about UFOs – including a radar visual case near Nottingham the previous April that had been kept top secret. At the one and only men-tion of the Llandrillo affair in my conversation with an RAF radar expert, silence descended for a few seconds, followed by a rapid change of subject. There may have been nothing to this, but it seemed odd at the time.

While almost everybody (even in ufology) forgot about Llandrillo, I later received a batch of material during the late 1970s that took it very seriously indeed. The origin of this information was a weird outfit calling itself APEN (Aerial Phenomena Enquiry Network). It never gave a contact address and always used pseudonyms, but it was a real nuisance in the UFO field between spring 1974 and 1981, when it faded from the scene. It briefly resurfaced during the Bentwaters/Woodbridge affair in 1983–84 (see pages 131–148), only to disappear again.

Aside from letters and documents, APEN sent out tape-recorded messages, established phone links with some investigators and even personal meetings with one man whom they chose as their reluctant go-between. The whole episode was unsavoury as the tapes contained Nazi war marches and other references to politics. APEN also got several people into trouble with the police via devious tactics which seemed only calculated to cause disruption. Yet it knew a phenomenal amount about key UFO figures. For instance, the day I moved house in February 1976 – with few yet aware of my new address and immediately after I had criticized APEN's tactics in a magazine article – I found a 'welcome to your new house' card greeting me. It bore the motto, 'Never call anyone bigger than yourself stupid.' Threats like this were not uncommon.

I wrote extensively on APEN in a series of articles for *The Unknown* in 1986. Nobody ever found out its true identity. The one and only time APEN discussed a specific UFO case was in connection with the Llandrillo affair. It did this first in a letter to me in the spring of 1974 and in such a vague way that I only realized in retrospect what they meant. APEN often spoke in riddles, such as one letter which said: 'Code 7A=Case no 174L 74-71/349 ST Classification now=Jasmine=clearance date 02 December 1974. All units concerned to co-operate fully with [Randles] on this one incident until further orders.'

Eventually APEN promised details on what it now termed 'the North Wales Landing' after it cleared 'Northern Control' (fictional leader names, silly bureaucracy, widespread postmarks, etc. were common APEN tactics). It used headed stationery, whose origin was traced, opening up a real can of worms designed to incriminate innocent people . . . but that's another story!

After several other false starts (including promises about

a 'Microbiological Report' on the case, which never arrived), a six-page dossier on the landing reached me via the usual anonymous sources. It was stamped with the personal approval of the APEN 'Supreme Commander' – one J.T. Anderson – apparently American (his alleged voice appeared on later tape messages). I did notice that Anderson used the dating 04.12 for 4 December, as customary in Britain, while Americans would habitually write 12.04 to indicate the same date. The report itself is said to be a preliminary on-site account by teletype from APEN's secret unit in the field. It is dated 24 January 1974 (the day following the crash) and refers to the site as merely Llan— with the remaining letters blacked out. Half the villages in Wales start with this prefix, but it is now clear they were referring to the then forgotten (and for most barely relevant) Llandrillo affair. It is also interesting that Bala tended to get most attention in media reports, being the nearest town of even modest size to the crash site; but not for APEN.

The account, in the usual overinflated style, is Mr W's, a witness about whom extensive information is given. Indeed, it was an impressive case file in that respect, assuming Mr W exists. I have deliberately kept specific details of him from this book, save to say that he was a former military officer living on the mountainside in a remote cottage, but everything APEN reported fitted what I later came to discover about him. At the time it was certainly not well known, even in ufology.

The account alleged that a UFO – 'Discoid, domed ball and tripod undercarriage, 4 portholes, 200 ft [61 m] by 50 ft [15 m] in size and polished metallic' – had come down on the 'hill known locally as a mountain' (as indeed it is). The field agent thought it was a 'contact (almost proven)' and recommended 'Time regression hypnosis', which in 1974 had never been carried out on a British case. The field officer requests further equipment to be sent to the landing site, including a 'Landrover (low wheel base), theodolite, stroboscope, infrared/ultra-violet sensors and five walky talkies.' Four other investigators were required, including one female. Such James Bond-style ufology, with 349 'agents' on tap, seems absurd, but even more fantastic was that Mr W was allegedly told by the aliens from the landed/crashed UFO to contact APEN alone. They even gave him the group's ex-directory phone number in order for him to do so!

Obviously, the most likely explanation is that this was all an elaborate hoax. However, its persistence for so many years and its curious nature make it a challenge. Moreover, it is decidedly curious that in seven years of communications, the one case that APEN took seriously was the one which, with hindsight, seems to have been of far more relevance than anybody spotted at the time. Indeed, it is hard to ignore the fact that APEN seems to have possessed credible data about it (as well as what seems patently absurd capabilities to follow up and suppress it) at a time when nobody knew anything – and cared even less – about what had taken place.

Also, the fact that the only other time APEN resurfaced was during the Bentwaters affair – the only other case which rivals Llandrillo in the past quarter century for its military importance in the UK – is again worth noting. Apen was again interested in that before most ufologists saw its significance. I was invited to clandestine meetings, in out of the way places, late at night which, to be honest – given the APEN track record – I simply refused to have any part in.

Almost 20 years later, a really dedicated ufologist, Margaret Fry, was able to learn the first direct testimony about this dramatic episode. Having 'retired', she moved to a village about 20 miles from the area. As a result of media appearances and lectures at a local college during 1993, she was approached by several first-hand witnesses to the still undiscussed affair. One woman had been working in a hotel at Bala in January 1974. She recalled the tremor well, because shelving fell down and glasses smashed. She also heard the explosion. She described how the police and army cordoned off the only proper road up into the Berwyn Mountains from Bala and the speculation that surrounded it. But, perhaps most interesting of all, she said that a group of strange men had arrived at the hotel a day or so later and stayed several days. They made trips to and from the mountain but avoided all questions about what they were doing up there. These men were not locals and they were noticed because they helped fill the hotel at a time when normally it was almost empty.

Another woman, in the course of reporting something else, told Margaret how she and her brother had driven their father to visit relatives in Llanderfel, a village midway between Llandrillo and Bala, in 'winter 1974'. Leaving late that night, they spotted an orange glow on top of the Berwyn Mountains to the west. They had to drive past the mountain on the way home and they were surprised to see many cars at the start of a road going into the hills. They tried to turn off the road to investigate, but they were immediately turned back by a group of soldiers. They heard talk of a UFO.

An almost identical story was given to Margaret by a young woman working in a printer's shop in Wrexham who saw that she was copying a UFO file (not one about this incident). The woman said that her mother had seen a glowing mass of light on the Berwyn Mountains in January 1974. She tried to get nearer but was turned away by the military. Sadly, despite requests, the mother has so far refused to talk to Margaret about this.

However, the best account collected so far comes from a nurse living at Llanderfel. She recalled the night of the explosion and earthquake and being telephoned by the police headquarters at Colwyn Bay and asked to assist at a plane crash near her home. She got her medical kit together and, since there was nobody to look after her teenage daughters, took them with her to the spot described by the police. The nurse took the B4391 road from Bala to Llangynog, which skirts the south of the Cader Bronwen area. There was no other traffic on it because it was around 10 o'clock on a winter's night. She took the track up towards the top of the range and came very close to something sitting on the ground that 'absolutely staggered' her. She described it as 'quite intact'; evidently it had not crashed, at least not in the way an aircraft would have done had it impacted on the mountainside. It was very large, circular and glowing orange. The nurse and her daughters were within a few hundred feet of it for 10 minutes and there was no possibility of mistaken identity. It was clearly a UFO.

Police and military forces, who had been even closer to the object, passed her on their way down the mountain. She explained why she was there and asked what was happening. Nobody answered her questions, except to say she would have to leave; no one unauthorized was allowed up there. So they escorted her down to the main road. Because she was afraid for her daughters' safety, she did not argue and left. To this day, she wonders what she saw up there. For several days afterwards, the road was sealed off. She heard complaints from local shepherds who were not even allowed to go up and tend to their flocks, which made them very angry. She is adamant that there was a massive cover-up of some still-unresolved incident on that barren hilltop. The facts suggest that she is right. Margaret Fry has supplied me with the names of all these witnesses. They are not anonymous sources, but I have decided to protect them from undue attention. That Margaret Fry has found these people by accident suggests that a concerted effort in this remote part of North Wales would pay dividends. Who knows how many other people have a piece to add to the jigsaw? It may not be too late to discover what really happened on the night the mountain exploded.

1977:
SAUCER OVER VICTOR ALERT

NATO has many strategic bases in Europe, including one at Aviano in north-eastern Italy. In the early hours of 1 July 1977, this was the scene of yet another military close encounter.

The case was investigated by Antonio Chiumiento, of the UFO group CUN, who lives close to the NATO base. Even so, it was not an easy story to follow up, because nothing was reported officially. However, it was also a difficult story for the authorities to hide completely, and rumours began to reach Chiumiento from a variety of sources. Then the eyewitnesses came forward. A key source was an Italian Air Force officer who acted as an intermediary and spoke with several of those on base who were involved, secretly relaying the information to Chiumiento.

On 1 July 1977, the base was closed for flying, since it was preparing for a major parade. But at 3 am a USAF guard spotted something strange directly above what was called 'Victor Alert', a well-secured hangar housing two jets requiring special protection. The object looked like a large spinning top, perhaps 45 m (150 ft) in diameter, hovering very low above the hangar, boldly defiant. On its upper surface was a dome. As it rotated, white, red and green lights and a loud buzzing or humming noise, like a huge swarm of bees, were emitted by the UFO.

Because it was spurning top security, as well as gravity, the guard immediately reported the matter. The base commander was brought in and a large detachment of air personnel was sent to the hangar. They surrounded the area, and then looked on. The radar officer, off duty because of the cancellation of flights, was recalled. Apparently, he did track the object towards the end of its appearance, although prior to that the base suffered a dramatic power loss: it was as if the

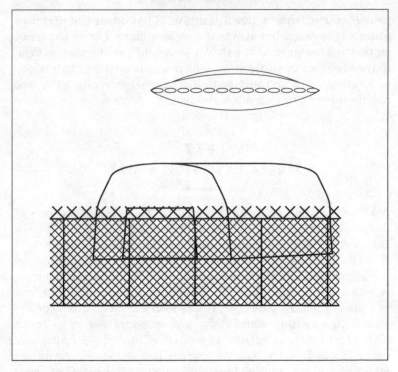

The UFO over the NATO base at Aviano, Italy.

UFO were demonstrating its technological superiority to the NATO forces by so brazenly ignoring this strict security zone.

According to Chiumiento's air force source, even NATO headquarters in Brussels was eventually involved, so seriously was the matter regarded. Although nothing was mentioned in the media about the affair, investigations around Aviano revealed that people outside the base had seen things that night.

Benito Manfre, an off-duty nightwatchman at Castello d'Aviano, told of being woken by his big sheepdog in the middle of the night. Going out to investigate, pistol in hand, Manfre saw the nearby NATO base suddenly plunged into darkness. Yet one spot (which Manfre did not then know was the Victor Alert area) had a huge white mass directly above it, almost on the ground. The dog continued to bark furiously, even though Manfre could hear no noise from the UFO. After a few minutes he saw it shoot away over the mountains. About 10 seconds after it had climbed skyward, the base burst into light again, and the sheepdog stopped barking.

Of course, this is not a crash or retrieval in the accepted sense of the term, but it was worth including a brief summary since it seems to form a pattern with other UFO cases – coming into direct confrontation with the military inside restricted air space. When asked about the event by investigators, the USAF did not try to deny it. It did not comment on the power loss, but merely said that the one-hour-long encounter was a misperception of the moon shining off some low cloud. Needless to say, Chiumiento found this conclusion difficult to swallow.

1979:
AIR CHASE ACROSS THREE UK COUNTIES

On 24 February 1979 my phone rang in the middle of the night. The caller was Mike Sacks, a tailor from east Lancashire, who had obtained my number via the Jodrell Bank Space Centre. He wanted to describe something that had just happened to him.

Mike and his wife were up late, looking after their son, who was ill with tonsillitis, when a dazzling object, awash in orange light, became visible through a window. It lit up the room as it fell slowly and silently from the sky over the Rossendale Valley – a rural, hilly area 30 km (20 miles) north of Manchester and so rich in sightings it is known locally as 'UFO alley'. Mike and his wife both saw the glow as it plunged downwards, then stopped dead in the sky and changed course in an instant, the light going out and revealing a superstructure comprising a blue arc of light and three reddish rings underneath. The object fell on to the ground. Mike thought that it had fallen into a disused quarry between Stacksteads and Bacup, behind his house. I knew the area well, having been born and raised in Stacksteads itself. The 8 km (5 miles) between here and Todmorden, just across the Yorkshire border, were regularly swamped with sightings, including what is probably the area's most famous incident of all: the spacenapping of police officer Alan Godfrey in 1980.

The time of the Stacksteads 'crash landing' had been just after 2 am. It was definitely not much later, since Mike called me right away. He said that he was going to get his brother's camera, leaving his wife to watch over the quarry. The UFO never came out. There was little I could do nearly 50 km (30 miles) away and without a car. I have always regretted that fact.

At about 2.45 am Mike went to the quarry with the loaded camera, hoping to get proof of the UFO. He was convinced it was there. However, the quarry appeared empty. But Mike was in a strange state of consciousness. Later, he described seeing a row of windows on the ground and a peculiar voice repeating in his mind 'Porta-cabin ... Porta-cabin', thus assuring him that these windows were nothing unusual and no big deal. But as dawn broke and he returned to the quarry, Mike realized that there were no portable workmen's huts in the quarry. There was nothing up there to explain what he had seen down below.

However, Mike had not been alone on his first visit to the quarry. While entering it, he met two figures silhouetted in the dark, torch beams blazing: policemen who had made the hazardous walk up the slopes. When interviewed later, they explained that at about 2.40 am, while Mike was making his way to the quarry, the two officers had then been on patrol along the valley road between Bacup and Rawtenstall. A strange bright light had floated over them and disappeared across the hills to the west. They did not get the impression that it was in trouble or preparing to land, yet, for no apparent reason, they decided to leave their car and walk to the isolated hillside.

That might have been the end of the story if the events in Rossendale were taken in isolation – although Mike Sacks did find others who had seen something in the valley that night, such as farmer Alf Kyme, out on the slopes with a cow in calf, who, with several farmhands, saw a dome-shaped mass surrounded by red rings drop towards the quarry. However, the story continued, further west. Indeed, pieces of it are still falling into place over 15 years later. Between 2.40 and 2.50 am, there were at least half-a-dozen reports made independently to UFO groups in Greater Manchester, west Lancashire and Merseyside, which described an orange ball of light. None of these reports described the silent structure seen by Mike and his wife 45 minutes earlier – several even referred to a loud roaring noise.

A firefighter, moonlighting as a taxi driver, was at Bryn, near Wigan, carrying a woman passenger. He tried to chase the thing westwards, but lost it. A police car in St Helens had a similar encounter. Nearer the coast, at Ormskirk, a courting couple had to jump from their car, fearing it was on fire when the interior turned orange. Overhead was the ball of flame streaking off towards the north-west. However, the most dramatic episode was at a caravan park at Scarisbrick, on the coast near Southport. Here, residents were shaken from their sleep by rattling doors and windows, and a roaring ball of red fire shot across, very low in front of them. The local MP, Robert Kilroy-Silk, reviewed the reports and decided to take action.

At first, the CAA (Civil Aviation Authority) made the obvious suggestion that the ball of light which nearly wrecked the trailer park was nothing more than a low-flying fighter jet using its afterburner to kick up speed. This should not have happened over a populated area with a lot of civil air traffic, but it might have been an accident. However, the CAA quickly withdrew the suggestion. The Ministry of Defence finally gave its position in a written statement which was a masterpiece of waffling. It confirmed that the USAF was involved in a 'special exercise' using F-111 jets from Upper Heyford in Oxfordshire; but it drew back from proposing that a straying USAF jet was to blame, simply allowing their statement to leave most people to draw that inference. I suspect that Kilroy-Silk accepted this as it stood; after all, no serious damage or injury had resulted. He took the matter no further. However, ufologists were not satisfied with this explanation.

Colonel Shrihofer, base commander at Upper Heyford, was very forthright. He checked his records, then said: 'Definitely not F-111s – that's official!' This firm statement was put to the MoD, which noted that there were certain 'avoidance areas', including where the sightings occurred; low flying did not happen there: another way to evade a straight answer. After continued pressure, the MoD finally bit the bullet and wrote to me about the idea that the USAF jet using its afterburner had caused the sightings, saying that 'clearly our suggestion was wrong. But then it was never put forward as an explanation in the first place.' Naturally, when official sources avoid questions, and even dangle red herrings in an attempt to mislead you, it suggests that something happened that they do not want you to know about. They must have been very relieved that an MP of the stature of Robert Kilroy-Silk did not have the full facts to press them all the way on this affair, for it might have had a serious effect on their cover-up.

But what was the MoD cover-up about? Before I compiled my first report on this case, I received a letter from a security guard on Blackpool central pier who had no knowledge of the other sightings. He gave me his story but I was unable to follow it up in detail until May 1994, when we met by chance and I took the opportunity to quiz him further.

He was on duty at about 2.45 am (in his letter he had said 3.15 am, but this was a mistake which he explained at our meeting by noting 'I was amazed that you knew the correct time. This convinced me more than anything that something really happened.'). Suddenly he felt what seemed like a violent swell, which was not unusual in the winter. Then a loud roaring passed overhead and he rushed out to see what was happening. The noise was caused by a jet aircraft to the south, shooting north-westwards across the Irish Sea. Above the water, heading out to sea, was an orange ball of light. He thought this was not the aircraft as the noise was separate

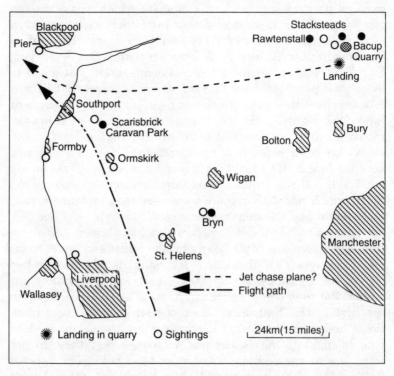

A map showing the February 1979 flightpath of an object over north-west England.

from it, but it may, perhaps, have been the jet's afterburner. Or it might have been the UFO. The guard also noticed a peculiar smell, like electrical arcing or very strong ozone (which usually results from ionization in the atmosphere from an electrical field linked to a UFO). The guard had given the wrong time because of what happened next. He stayed outside, composing what to report on the matter. Neither the orange ball nor the jet aircraft returned. But, at about 3.15 am, he saw another very odd thing: a series of white lights rising from the sea to the south, at least 1.5 km (1 mile) offshore. They appeared to be separate but in unison, perhaps half-a-dozen in all. They spiralled up into the sky and then vanished. This guard had spent many years on the pier, but he had never seen anything like this before or since. The combination of the two strange events within half an hour suggest that they were related.

Putting together what is known about this case, a very interesting scenario can be drawn up. Mike Sacks and his wife, the farmer and others in Rossendale, mention a clearly structured object falling into the Stacksteads quarry at about 2 am. It was never seen to leave, unless that is what the two police officers saw about 35 minutes later and Mike was somehow 'prevented' from witnessing it; if so, it left heading westwards. Between 2.40 and 2.50, an object like a jet fighter using afterburners defied all the rules and shot across Lancashire and Merseyside from the south, on an intercept course with the thing that left the quarry. It seems a fair assumption that this is exactly what happened. The RAF or USAF (or both) knew about the Stacksteads quarry UFO and a jet was sent in hot pursuit of it when it departed westwards. The caravan park at Scarisbrick just happened to be in the way. The security guard at Blackpool apparently saw the jet tear off out across the Irish Sea, presumably in pursuit of the radar target. But did the fighter ever catch it? We may have to wait until the year 2009 before the '30 year rule' protecting official documents releases data and lets us find out.

On the other hand, did the UFO hide under the sea to avoid capture? It would be fascinating if that is what the guard saw 30 minutes later: the strange craft finally departing when the coast was clear.

CHAPTER SEVEN

COSMIC
CONSPIRACIES

In the 1980s, as new documents were released under the
American FoI Act, doubts escalated about what the government
actually knew.

Officially, the story was that it had ended all interest in UFOs in
1969, when it closed Project Blue Book. The documents,
however, revealed a different story. A memo from a high-
ranking USAF officer (Brigadier-General C. Bolender) in
October 1969 concerned the Blue Book closure. It noted that
important cases (those affecting national security) had never
appeared in the Blue Book files. Instead, they were dealt with
elsewhere, something that would continue despite the public
being told to the contrary.

The CIA also released documents which showed that between
April and July 1976 – and probably ever since – it had staff in its
department of scientific analysis working on UFO data and, as
it put it, 'monitoring UFO reporting channels'. The CIA interest
appeared to be technology and propulsion systems and overseas
progress in making breakthroughs in these areas.

Even the ultra-secret NSA (National Security Agency), with
satellite tracking systems the envy of the world, has hundreds
of files on UFOs, but it refused to release them, even when
taken to the highest courts in the land by FoI activists between
1979 and 1982. That this refusal may have simply been tied to its
desire not to reveal methods of tracking is rejected when we see
that it even refused to reveal the content of messages without
any reference to how such messages were intercepted. Indeed, a
top-security-cleared judge who oversaw the NSA's case was not
even allowed access to the documents. All he got was a 21-page
statement justifying why they had to stay secret; that
statement itself was then classified top secret and covered up!
Eventually, a version of it was squeezed out on appeal, although
most of it was lost beneath a sea of censors' ink. However, it did
show that the NSA regarded the UFO evidence as 'surprise
material' and its expert staff had produced several long papers,
although the titles, of course, were considered top secret!

In the face of such mounting evidence, one can see why ufologists came to believe that significant data were lurking behind the protestations of official ignorance, and that this data might include first-hand knowledge of the UFOs and their occupants, possibly accrued via retrievals, such as at Roswell. The hunt was on to find the 'smoking gun' – files that proved this fact. As yet, it has been an elusive chase. Matters have been complicated by the release of a host of spurious files alongside *bona fide* documentation under FoI. The MJ–12 affair is the best example of the authorities trying to create confusion in the UFO community.

MJ–12 (MJ for Majestic) was said to be a secret team created after Roswell in 1947, composed of high-level intelligence and scientific personnel. The so-called MJ–12 briefing file was sent on a roll of film by an anonymous source to Bill Moore, key investigator into the Roswell case, and colleagues Jaime Shandera and Stanton Friedman. It purported to be part of a large document briefing President Truman on the matter, prior to his taking office in 1952. But most of its detail and appendices were missing.

The documents were not made public until English researcher Tim Good published them in *Above Top Secret* in May 1987 – to the surprise of his American colleagues, who did not know that he had received a copy via another anonymous source. This left Moore with no choice but to reveal what he knew about the matter, and so the debate began.

Doubts rose about the authenticity of the Truman signature, and what seemed to be a match was found by sceptics. Far from being good news, an existing identical signature undermined the credibility of the papers, since no two signatures are ever exactly the same, unless they are copies. The arguments still rage. While some questions remain, many ufologists think that the files were produced by sources unknown and fed to investigators, such as Moore and Good, in the hope that they would make them public. This would discredit the whole idea of crashed UFOs if the truth about them later emerged. But who would want to do this? The thought was mooted of a government source, perhaps worried by the FoI revelations.

I myself was offered what may have been the MJ–12 files complete with their appendices (over 500 pages in all) before they were publicly revealed. That was in October 1986, just as I was completing *The UFO Conspiracy*. My source was a British military officer who reputedly got them via Wright Patterson air force base. Apparently a serviceman had found them on his computer there, printed them out and then been caught. He got them out of the country before they were taken from him. I met the officer, along with Peter Hough. We received a detailed account of the files' contents, but never saw them, assuming indeed, that they existed. Later, when our source failed to show up to pass on the files, we were told that he had been held at a military base, where he handed over the dossier. By then Peter and I had conducted background checks on him. Whether that provoked his response is a matter of speculation, but we could not accept these files at face value.

Shortly after these events, Tim Good was given, and quickly published, the MJ–12 papers and the furore over their nature rapidly grew. We may never know if this was all coincidence, nor discover the truth about the MJ–12 affair. However, I am reasonably certain that no ufologist was involved in any trickery. If this were a hoax, then someone outside the UFO community was trying to dupe UFO researchers for some reason.

Soon after, Bill Moore shocked the UFO world by admitting that he himself had been ensnared into a government disinformation campaign in which bogus documents about a mythical 'Project Aquarius' were given to another American ufologist by vague intelligence sources. The ufologist was then monitored as his credibility collapsed about him. Moore simply reported back on what was happening, in exchange for what he believed was true information fed from 'deep throat' government sources trying to break the cover-up. Moore's astonishing admission of his small part in this disinformation process was a brave act. Many colleagues were horrified by what he claimed. But, if such a plan was initiated within intelligence circles, it illustrates the lengths to which some people in the US government are going to cloud the retrieval evidence. Any amazing 'secret' documents mysteriously finding their way into the public domain now must be considered suspect. Of course, maybe that was the whole point: if you get even ufologists to distrust what seems like red-hot documents, then how seriously will they take any real files that leak by chance into the public arena?

1980:
THE RENDLESHAM FOREST AFFAIR

The ultimate game of information–disinformation–misinformation seems to have involved the Rendlesham Forest incident in late December 1980. More has probably been written on this important case than any other in British ufology. Like Roswell before it, it is also attracting plans for a big-budget, Hollywood movie, this time with an ace conspiracy-story director reported to be interested.

This is a case to which I am very attached having first become involved in January 1981, a few days after it happened. I was the first writer to mention it in public, in an article for *Flying Saucer Review* that same spring. At that point, it was just a mass of often conflicting rumours and tall tales, which showed little hope of ever being resolved into a coherent story. Eventually, I went on to write two books about the matter. In the first, *Sky Crash*, I worked with two locals, Brenda Butler and Dot Street, who collected the gaggle of tales circulating in the local villages during the days and weeks after the event. *From Out of the Blue* was published more recently. It was the culmination of a decade of research, so sensitive that I had to publish in the USA!

The case has attracted a number of media presentations abroad, as witnesses have gradually freed themselves from military constraints. These include a 90-minute dramatization in Japan and top US shows, such as *Unsolved Mysteries* and *Sightings*, which recreated events. However, there has been relatively little coverage in Britain, although this changed somewhat when I worked on the series *Strange but True?*

With eyewitnesses coming forward to appear on TV or planning their own book about it, it is hard for people now to realize what it was like between 1981 and 1983, when Brenda, Dot and I were three voices crying in the wilderness – shunned by nearly all our colleagues, who frankly did not even believe that there was any story to investigate.

Indeed, in 1982, one group of ufologists even published a report attacking us for taking the matter seriously, claiming that it had no substance. One leading British sceptic has also gone on record for calling it 'a ghastly embarrassment to ufology'. What is so controversial about this case, that we were challenged for upsetting the ufology apple-cart?

It is impossible to offer more than a summary of the evidence, because over 50 witnesses are involved. Undoubtedly, it is now the best attested case of an alleged UFO crash outside the USA. It also has official backing, in the form of documentation, but none of that appeared for the first three years, during which data collection was a nightmare.

The case did not achieve any publicity, even in the local Press, during the time it happened. The first Press reference came in May 1981, when I mentioned it in passing in an interview for the London *Evening Standard*. This, and a local BBC interview Dot Street gave later that summer, were both largely ignored. There is some speculation that 'D' notices were imposed by the government to prevent further discussion. However, I suspect it is more likely that the lack of any hard facts, stonewalling tactics from the MoD and military, plus general confusion, meant that no editor would risk publishing material about it.

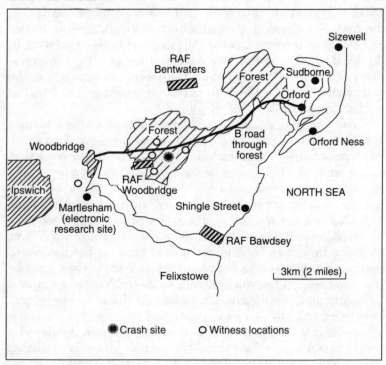

A map locating the UFO crash in Rendlesham Forest, Suffolk, in December 1980.

It must also be remembered that the area where this event occurred is very similar, in many respects, to the New Mexico desert, since it is the home of numerous military facilities, including the two NATO air bases, Bentwaters and Woodbridge, then staffed entirely by American servicemen. It also involves unknown laboratories on Orford Ness island (where the NSA had experimental units, officially researching 'over the horizon' radar), an electronics site at Martlesham Heath (where rumours abound about interesting experimental activity), plus a large and very sensitive RAF site, Bawdsey Manor, where security is tighter than at most other bases. In addition, this is the area where radar was first developed during the 1930s and in World War 2 the entire village of Shingle Street was evacuated, and all census records ended, for reasons that remain mysterious to this day. Finally, one of the most controversial nuclear facilities in the UK (Sizewell) is right in the middle of the action.

It is difficult to imagine a more sensitive area in the whole of northern Europe, which makes a mockery of the official claim, by both British and American governments, that records on the affair comprise just one sheet of paper – a summary report to the MoD from the American deputy commander at Bentwaters.

Just after Christmas 1980, Brenda Butler, who had investigated ghostly happenings in and around Suffolk for some years, was contacted by an American friend who was a security police officer at the twin bases of Bentwaters and Woodbridge (run as one unit, but separated by a mile or so of dense forest bisected only by the small Orford to Woodbridge B road). The friend, Steve, had special duties, normally involving drug patrols. However, he said that in the early hours of 26 December, he and two other guards had been sent into Tangham Woods, part of the forest 0.75 km (½ mile) from the Woodbridge end of the runway. There had been reports of a big light crashing down from the sky into the trees. When the guards reached the spot, they were astonished to find a disc-shaped craft on tripod legs on the ground. They immediately called for help. During the next couple of hours, senior personnel came out, reputedly some interrupting a Christmas night party. This included the wing-commander for the entire unit, Brigadier-General Gordon Williams (who has usually remained silent but, when put on record, denied that he was present).

133

Steve reported that several small aliens – with large heads, greyish skins and about 1 m (3½ ft) tall – were hovering in mid-air in a shaft of light suspended under the craft. It looked as if they were attempting to repair their craft, which had been damaged by the impact. A senior officer (said by Steve to be Williams, a claim disputed by most other eyewitnesses) was using sign language to try to communicate with them. Troops swarmed out and cordoned off the craft, thus preventing non-military personnel coming into the woods and witnessing this amazing sight. Given that this was private land, owned by the British Forestry Commission, and that an adjacent field was grazed by a farmer, there was some danger of this episode being witnessed by civilians, even at 2 am. The entire proceedings were supposedly filmed by the US military.

There are more than a few similarities with the reported events at Holloman air base in New Mexico, where an 'expected' alien landing was guarded and filmed by the USAF. How relevant that is, remains to be seen. However, here we had only an unsupported statement by a man who, typical of retrieval witnesses, insisted upon total anonymity. Indeed it was three years before Brenda even shared his real name with me.

As it stands, this story would not have thrown the world into a frenzy. Right from the start, I kept wondering why this obviously security-conscious man would relate this story to a UFO buff and how, if it had happened in the manner described and with so many people involved, it had been contained. Steve did explain about the debriefings and threats against those who witnessed it; how some young servicemen needed counselling, so shaken were they by the events; also how some of the more talkative people had been quickly despatched to bases around the world to diminish the chances of a leak – apparently a common practice by the military when a cover-up is involved.

Unsurprisingly, nobody in the UFO world was falling over themselves to investigate this story. However, there was a reason why I was not one of the many sceptics when I first heard the tale via Brenda's colleague, Dot Street, in February 1981. I was already chasing an independent rumour about what was obviously the same case – the overlaps were too close to be coincidence.

The story had come to me via Paul Begg, a sceptical writer whose association with UFOs was minimal. We respected each other's work and, as he could do nothing with the tale himself,

he suggested that I research it. It had come to him in an equally unimpressive fashion, from an acquaintance in a pub, 80 km
(50 miles) north of the forest, in a village near Norwich. The
source, David, was a civilian radar officer at Watton, a joint
military/civilian base, also sometimes known as Eastern
Radar, that covers traffic in the northern part of East Anglia.
David was off duty on the night in question but he was present
the next day, during a similar incident.

He told me that on 27 December (although there is reason
to believe that it was actually the night before), an object was
tracked crossing the coast north of Lowestoft. It was an
unscheduled target and the usual procedures were followed.
Other radar bases had tracked it, but Watton lost the signal as
it disappeared off screen in the vicinity of Bentwaters base.
Watton could not tell if it had simply vanished or fallen from
the sky below their radar coverage, so there was some communication with Bentwaters about the matter.

This would have been the end of the story, just another
curious anomaly tracked by Watton. However, about two days
later, when David was present, some intelligence officers
arrived from the USAF. Watton had no USAF presence, so this
was unusual. Moreover, they came to take the radar recordings for several nights just after Christmas and justified this
step by telling a fantastic story. That story, as passed on to me
by David, was almost identical to the one Steve had told
Brenda days before. They wanted to see the radar recordings
because Watton might have tracked a UFO that crash-landed
outside Woodbridge base; senior personnel had gone there,
some from a party, and a commanding officer had communicated with little aliens. David provided me with some additional information. The entire episode had been tape-recorded
'live' by an officer from the base and a truck and portable
lights used to illuminate the area had suffered strange impe-
dence.

When I first heard this account, it was mid-January, less
than a month after the events had reputedly occurred. I was
over 400 km (250 miles) away, without transport and not
inclined to rush down to what was a very hard place to reach
by public transport. Moreover, I had never heard of Brenda
Butler or Dot Street, so I had no idea that they were in possession of a matching story from an eyewitness on Woodbridge
base.

I followed it up from a distance as best I could, but Watton and Bentwaters were silent on the matter. Indeed, it was almost ten years before Watton broke that silence and then the base commander, Squadron-Leader E.E. Webster, merely confirmed that their log recorded a discussion with Bentwaters that weekend about an alleged UFO, not whether they had actually tracked anything. Indeed, they said: 'All radio and radar recordings from the time have long since been disposed of.' Of course – presumably, these were given to the US government!

I also asked, in my capacity as investigations co-ordinator, for two colleagues, Peter Warrington (an expert on radar cases) and Kevin McClure (whose field was rumour proliferation), to assess whether the matter had any substance and was thus worth pursuing. Both soon gave up since there was so little hard data for them to work with. But then I heard about the Butler/Street version of the story, given to them from a source on the base. Could two so identical tales crop up so quickly and 80 km (50 miles) apart, unless something had really taken place? At least, the case was now worthy of further exploration.

It was late in 1981 before I became thoroughly involved, deciding to compile a case file from Brenda and Dot about their local investigations. These two women were hot on chasing up leads, but they had little experience of documenting their evidence. I wanted to preserve what they had uncovered as some kind of permanent record and did so in 1982 via a report to BUFORA and then a series of articles for *The Unexplained*. Then I wrote a book with Brenda and Dot during the following year. It appeared in 1984 as *Sky Crash*, but it was a mass of confusion, because this case was near impossible to piece together without any kind of official aid and with most military witnesses still too scared to talk.

Brenda and Dot had done quite a lot with the civilian population, but their scattered evidence was fragmentary. For instance, they had reports from Arthur Smekle, a travelling salesman passing on the Orford B road, who saw the object fall into the forest; the Webb family, returning from a Christmas party near Martlesham, saw something similar; and a courting couple then on the edge of the woods gave them an account of the UFO fall and the way the base sprang into life suddenly in immediate response.

Then there was the forestry worker, James Brownlea, who had discovered a huge hole smashed through the pine trees, 6 to 9 m (20 to 30 ft) up, as well as clear evidence that something had impacted heavily on the ground in the clearing underneath, leaving a set of indentations. This discovery was made a few days into January 1981. Brownlea reported the find immediately and, when he arrived for work next morning, found that part of the forest was already being felled by his co-workers. This area was due for felling later that winter, but this response seemed unduly swift and conveniently localized. Within a couple of days – before any ufologist got there – the site was an open field, devoid of any tree growth and with all trace evidence thus obscured.

The investigators also found locals, including another forestry worker, who recalled two men probing the site on 1 January 1981 – two weeks before (according to both the British and American governments' version of events) the Bentwaters base finally sent a one-page memo to the MoD, first reporting the matter. These visitors appeared to be from the British government and seemingly knew all about the case. Other sources alleged that they even took plaster casts of the marks in the forest. Whoever these visitors were, they seemed quite content that the Forestry Commission knew nothing about an alleged 'air crash', logically pointing out to these 'officials' that no aircraft could have crashed into a pine forest and failed to leave wreckage.

Then there was a civilian electrician, called in during the weekend after Christmas from far away to repair the Woodbridge runway lights at the edge of the forest. Clearly, these had been hit from the air. He was held under armed guard as he worked in an otherwise remote part of the base where such precautions are normally not enforced. This spot is in plain view, right beside a track that I have since walked on several times without being disturbed.

However, the most important eyewitness was probably Gordon Levett. He and his family lived in an isolated house at Sudbourne, on the edge of the woods. He was putting his dog into an outside kennel to guard the property for the night, when he saw the UFO approach from the coast. It was like an upturned mushroom glowing phosphorescent. Hovering briefly overhead, it then plunged out of sight, in the direction of Woodbridge. Next day, the Levetts' dog was taken ill. Soon it was dead.

On their own, these and other stories were almost inconsequential. However, all of them were reported during the first few weeks of 1981 at a time when nothing had been published about the case anywhere – in or out of UFO circles, let alone the local Press. So these people had no context into which to relate their stories. There were rumours in the pubs about a UFO crash, but Brenda and Dot's sleuthing had effectively established that there was a series of interlocking tales, dependent on clear, first-hand testimony, that something definitely had occurred. The duo also had a few calls from the twin bases – usually anonymous airmen saying that they wanted to report what had occurred without fear of being caught. Sometimes clandestine meetings were set up. These stories often added new, but logical, perspectives (for example, one man from the motor pool who saw Jeeps being despatched with great haste in the middle of the night). However, there were others that wanted to offer theories, for example, that the UFO was 'really' a secret military helicopter that had gone wrong, or a missile carelessly discarded by a passing plane. More than likely these airmen were simply passing on stories from the base, which was a seething mass of talk by this time.

Indeed, Brenda's initial source, Steve, further reported how there had been several UFO sightings in the week after the first episode, partly because airmen and their families camped out in the forest and even staged 'skywatching' parties around New Year.

This multiplicity of events and the fact that witnesses could be referring to any one of up to a dozen different incidents (and, we soon learnt that there were three principal sightings) created immense confusion. Data seemed to conflict. We could not even establish what the correct dates were, and Steve himself changed his story from 26 to 27 December for the night he was involved; although (thanks to Watton) we do now know for sure that the third of the primary sightings (but not the one that was tape-recorded) occurred at about 3 am on 28 December and the other two were on the two preceding nights. The main 'crash' was around 2 am on 26 December, although the official report to the MoD and all subsequent British and American government references to it wrongly state 27 December!

No doubt, some of the stories uncovered by the two women were unrelated anecdotes and we were criticized (for example, over a story they told about effects on their car engine while driving through the woods, or a sighting they made near the base which appears to have been a bright planet, not a UFO).

138

However, I felt that they had established a *prima facie* case that something had occurred, even if, in the absence of any documentation, hardly any other ufologist agreed with me.

The two women did try to obtain this documentation. They bravely marched on to Bentwaters base to see Squadron-Leader Donald Moreland about the case. Moreland was a kind of British overseer, as the bases were RAF property being leased to the US government as part of their NATO duties (and, indeed, they were returned by the USA in 1993 after the ending of the Cold War saw them vacate many European bases). This was an extraordinary plan for mid-February 1981. Moreland saw them and started to talk about the case, apparently assuming that they were from the British government, because they did not specify who they were, merely that they wanted to discuss the UFO landing. Moreland quickly realized his error and sent them packing, saying he could only talk if they got permission in writing from the MoD in London. But he had by his actions confirmed the reality of the case and left Brenda and Dot (and later myself, when I met him) convinced that we were right not to give in about this affair.

In fact, two years later, after I had met the squadron-leader in his office, we realized that Moreland's error was forgivable. He had urged the deputy base commander, Lieutenant-Colonel Charles Halt, to submit an official report to the MoD. Halt was not happy with the lack of interest by either the British or American government in what had taken place, but Moreland persuaded him that it was courtesy to file this account with the host country. It had been sent three weeks after the first incident, just a month before Brenda and Dot visited the squadron-leader. Moreland was sure some government official would come to make enquiries after receiving that file, and so he was ready to provide more data. Then Brenda and Dot appeared at his office, knowing all about a case that he assumed had been kept out of the public eye. Naturally, he concluded they had to be from the government.

Brenda wrote to the MoD, but she was given the runaround and a completely non-committal reply, which waffled on about investigating UFOs for 'defence' purposes, but which failed to mention the Rendlesham case at all – despite this being the entire substance of the ufologist's letter of enquiry. Being rather cynical of the MoD and their 'cover-up', Brenda left it at that. However, as she and Dot continued to hunt for more witnesses (in particular trying to find a farmer whom several sources had mentioned, because his cattle were spooked by the thing as it fell into the forest), I found that I now had a role to play, even at a distance. So I renewed the attack on the MoD and tried to lull them into submission.

It was a tough fight, but in October 1982 I made a mini-breakthrough when it promised to release files on UFO cases for the first time in 30 years. I had to keep this news secret for three months, to avoid jeopardizing this historic decision. However, from January 1983 it started to release assorted sighting data to me. Twice I asked for the file on the Rendlesham case. Twice they avoided the question and sent me cases from elsewhere instead, perhaps hoping this would deflect my attention.

Then, in February 1983, two remarkable things occurred. One of the senior officers from the base gave his second-hand account to *OMNI* of what some of the men had seen in the forest. It was an amazing move. Moreland was cited in the article, explaining with some gusto how he had put Brenda and Dot off the trail. Yet both men agreed that there *had* been a close encounter in the forest: a strange object had been seen and nobody appeared to know what it was. *OMNI* had called me and I was quoted as expressing a note of caution. By this point I was rather concerned about the way in which the 'spaceship' story was finding its way into the public domain. Why, for instance, would those USAF intelligence officers tell civilian radar operators at Watton the whole story about crashed UFOs, aliens, contact with the base commander and the like? What possible need to know did they have? It runs contrary to all notion of secrecy in this book and was almost as if this tale was told in the full realization that it would leak to ufologists. Was it intended to make the story seem absurd and so scuttle any serious investigation?

Brenda's source, 14 years later, has never gone public, even though at least a dozen of the witnesses (including deputy commander Halt and other personnel senior to Steve) have now appeared in front of the cameras. Perhaps he is still afraid to talk, but none of the witnesses that I have met (some of which should have been with Steve in the forest) has ever suggested the real name of Steve to me when other names are mentioned. Yet Steve, a base security officer, told the same elaborate story about the case directly to a ufologist within a few days of the events. Few of the other witnesses who have come forward support the claim about aliens repairing their crashed spaceship and contact with a senior officer. However, they all do support the story that something weird was seen in the forest, even while rejecting large parts of the version fed out to Brenda Butler and to myself by two quite different sources. The versions we heard immediately after the sightings were guaranteed to place the case in only one possible context: if our sources were telling the truth, then their version offers little alternative to an alien retrieval operation where the USAF helped the aliens to escape!

Clearly, whichever way we evaluate this case, the fantastic status of the episode, pandering straight to the desires of the UFO movement (and almost, thus, guaranteed repudiation from any serious media source), was set from the very start. As I told *OMNI* magazine, I could not help wondering if a disinformation game was not afoot. Maybe somebody wanted the 'spaceship' story to take hold in the hope that it would trivialize a more mundane – if disturbing – truth and ensure that this was effectively hidden.

I have never met Steve or any of the intelligence staff who gave their story to the Watton radar officers. I may be misjudging them and, if so, I apologize; they could just be telling the truth as they saw it, unafraid of repercussions. But in 1983 I was beginning to have self-doubts about whether I was being duped into acting as a pawn in a much bigger game.

The *OMNI* colonel, who has never spoken about the case in public since that one interview in 1983, helped to ensure that the UFO orientation of the case was secure in people's minds, even in my own. The story he and Moreland told, of a strange craft but no aliens, was eminently plausible.

Almost at the same time, an airman called Larry Warren (then using a pseudonym 'Art Wallace') approached ufologists Barry Greenwood and Larry Fawcett in New England and told them how, aged 19, he had been stationed at Bentwaters and described his role in the story. This included him being handpicked by a senior officer, taken out to the site in the forest and watching as the aspirin-shaped UFO sat on the ground surrounded by mist. A series of wonderful, reality-challenging experiences followed, but he did not refer to any aliens, until later, when hypnotically regressed by Dr Fred Max, a few inferences about alien contact emerged.

Barry Greenwood had read my articles on the case and he knew right away what Larry Warren was discussing (although Warren claimed not then to have read my work). The airman established his credentials, proving he was on Bentwaters base at the time and alleging that he was sent home (after being caught calling trans-Atlantic to his mother about the case) and an honourable discharge was then engineered a few months later. Warren has been the most consistently verbal witness, giving lectures in the USA, appearing in the first big media story (during October 1983) and as active as ever a decade later. It was to be much longer before anyone else spoke out.

In 1984 and 1985 Ray Boeche and Scott Colborne tracked down and interviewed two further witnesses, who were very reluctant to talk. Their stories were consistent with what we knew, but added plenty of fascinating new details about rainbow light shows, the involvement of the British police, photographs that were taken at the site, and so forth. Neither referred to any aliens. I spent some time with one of these witnesses in Arizona in 1989. I am sure he was presenting an honest and objective account.

Some of the other military witnesses (of at least 20 who seem to have been directly involved) banded together in an unofficial pact to talk only when they were free of air force connections. A few spoke for the first time in 1992 and others are gradually coming forward. Three faced the cameras in Britain late in 1994. I suspect that most are biding their time, waiting for the right vehicle to present their joint account to the public in such a way that it will be utterly convincing.

Two months after the *OMNI* story, in April 1983, the MoD suddenly wrote to me and admitted that the case was genuine. Of course, now that one of its squadron-leaders had admitted that in public, it had little choice. I was told that it involved 'unusual lights', that 'no explanation was ever forthcoming' and that there was no possibility of it being a smoke-screen to hide something else. All of which seemed explicit enough.

As I swapped this breakthrough with Barry Greenwood in Massachusetts, he was using the FoI Act to press for documentation based on Larry Warren's testimony. A few days after my letter, the USAF issued a similar admission to his team that there had indeed been sightings near Woodbridge base.

These two dramatic turnarounds were most welcome after years of denial, but I wanted more. The MoD had started to release files. Now I had its admission that there was a case to answer, so I requested that file. It never came. A year later I worked with a respected journalist for the *Guardian* newspaper, who featured a story about my battle to retrieve MoD data. He also tried to get the MoD file on Bentwaters, despite being told by it to just specify a date and location in his article. In any case, we already had the file by other means by then – as the MoD well knew. Yet still it failed to release it to one of Britain's most reputable newspapers. It was just one piece of paper – the report that Halt sent, on Moreland's advice, in January 1981 to the British government. The MoD has always since insisted that it is the only documentation on the case.

In June 1983, nine months before the *Guardian* story, this so-called 'Halt memo' was released under FoI to Greenwood and his team. In its covering letter, the USAF said it had destroyed its own copy and it had got this one from the MoD in London! Despite the fact that I had been arguing rationally for its release with my own government for two years, I could only get hold of it through an American citizen.

In August 1983, Brenda and I took this document to Whitehall and presented ourselves at the door of the MoD. I told the armed guards that I had a file the government had constantly denied to me and which I had obtained via America. I might be contravening the Official Secrets Act by possessing it, so what should I do, especially as I now intended to publish it? After a long wait, Pam Titchmarsh, then head of the relevant MoD department, came down and we spent an hour discussing the case. She looked clearly edgy. She admitted the file seemed like the one the MoD had, but denied having knowledge about the case other than what was contained within it.

The Halt memo discusses three separate events, starting with the landing of a small craft on the first night, moving into the discovery of ground traces with excess radiation readings, involving animal interference, and describing another encounter witnessed by 'numerous base personnel', which are said to include deputy base commander Halt himself. The report makes no reference to aliens, tape-recording or filming of the site, taking of samples from the damaged area or of radar trackings. It was written 17 days after the first sighting, but it gives no indication that there has, by that point, been any investigation, such as that alleged by foresters and farmers who saw the two British men probing the forest more than a week before Halt penned this memo.

Yet, despite Pam Titchmarsh's denial that there were any additional data on the case, she still knew all about the radar story, when I raised the matter. She claimed the radar readings did not correlate with the UFO landing. Then I pointed out that the Halt memo did not mention radar at all and she herself had just told us she had done no checking into the case and had no other records to peruse even if she had wanted to do further research. So, I asked, how could she know so much about one incident that happened long before she had started her present job and nearly three years before this meeting. She had an answer. By sheer coincidence radar staff had a few days earlier given her department a briefing on how to deal with UFO cases if there ever were a correlated radar target. Even though this 1980 event was not such a case, the radar staff had used it as an example.

Within a few weeks, I spoke to Squadron-Leader Moreland and he told me that there should be at least one other file with the MoD – his covering letter sent with Halt's memo. Ten years later, despite appeals, the MoD has never released – or even admitted to possessing – that document.

In the USA, similar brick walls were struck. Under the FoI Act, the government denied that there were any other documents about the case other than the Halt memo. Appeals for photographs, films, samples and the tape-recording that most of the witnesses (including Halt in private) had talked about, were all met with official denials. No such things existed.

Two years later, Ray Boeche did squeeze some additional documents out under FoI. These turned out to be mostly teletype messages discussing FoI appeals for this missing hard evidence. There were also interdepartment discussions about how to handle the media reaction to *Sky Crash*, although they were fortunate in that this book never even made it to the USA. Several further documents were denied under FoI. Boeche appealed and got only one of them – a teletype message in which the operator plays a joke (typing a row of UFO images on top!) and where frustration pours out and the operator appears to say to colleagues in the USAF that they have to come up with an explanation, almost irrespective of their true feelings on the matter.

Just as *Sky Crash* was about to appear, but too late to include any mention in the book, the former base commander at Bentwaters (then resident in the USA) released a tape-recording to British investigators. This was said to have been made in the forest in 1980 and, subsequent investigation showed, contained the voices of various senior personnel, including Halt (who was by now promoted to full base commander back at Bentwaters). The long-sought-after tape, which the US government had categorically denied existed, reaffirmed many of the details in the Halt memo and added new features, for example, a beam of light projecting down to the ground and the electrical interference on military equipment in the forest. The obvious distress of the airmen who were confronting this nightmare becomes clear as the sighting progresses. This seems to rule out any suspicion that this tape is anything but genuine. It lasts 18 minutes, but it spans several hours of real time in the early hours of either 27 or 28 December. We do not know if it is complete. Whatever the case, this is a unique piece of UFO evidence, all the more significant because it seems to prove the US government has lied under an FoI Act request. Could they really not have known about this tape which was released by a USAF base?

The recording clearly describes the taking of photographs by an officer from the disaster-preparedness team on base. Also it notes how samples were gathered from the ground and trees, and other evidence garnered at the site. These extra pieces of hard evidence were also appealed for – and denied – along with the tape under 1983 and 1984 FoI Act requests. To this day none of this material has been released, although belief is strong among witnesses that some of it still exists somewhere. In any case, the US government denial clearly cannot be trusted, even though telling untruths in response to FoI Act requests is illegal.

So what happened in Rendlesham Forest over that series of nights? We may never know for certain.

The sceptics entered the fray in 1983 and quickly 'solved' the case, without, I might add, interviewing a single witness. Indeed, in a 1994 book, *The UFO Mystery: Solved*, one of these sceptics appears to express amazement that Dot Street and I used money from the *News of the World* front-page story about the case to scour the world tracking down leads and travelling to interview witnesses. Yet this was the only reasonable thing to do if we were to have any hope of solving this case. It cost both Dot and me dear in terms of our personal relationships.

According to the sceptics, the UFO first seen was a bright meteor. This attracted airmen into the forest where, disorientated, they saw a lighthouse beacon shining through trees. Other UFOs that night were just bright stars. The ground traces later discovered were made by a rabbit; although the sceptics have so far avoided mentioning how rabbits leapt 6 m (20 ft) off the ground and smashed a hole through the pine tree canopy – clearly described by Colonel Halt on the tape and, three years before this was released, in identical detail when found by forestry-worker James Brownlea.

None of the witnesses I have interviewed regards the light-house theory as anything but absurd, yet to the sceptics it is case closed. Mind you, they do disagree about whether the source is the Orford Ness lighthouse or the Shipwash lightship. One sceptic, on a masterful TV presentation, even explained it as a police car, despite the police records (actually shown on the programme) indicating that they went out to the forest in order to investigate the report of the UFO. Think about that for a moment, then figure out how the UFO can be the police car called out into a dense forest to respond to the report of a UFO, which was the police car . . .

Of course, the favourite theory of the ufologists is that this was an alien UFO, with or without extraterrestrials, that crashed into the forest near a NATO air base and was wit-nessed by many USAF officers and men before it departed. Against this is the worrying manner in which this theory was almost force-fed to ufologists from the start.

From the witnesses I have talked with, I have little doubt that these men did see something remarkable: a weird phe-nomenon full of lights, misty forms, with elements of electrical fields, animal disturbance, physical energies and mind distor-tion. These men all saw something beyond their comprehen-sion. Very possibly this was a UFO in its truest 'alien' sense: a strange phenomenon, either some kind of unexplained nat-ural energy that can scramble the brainwaves at close proxim-ity, or the product of an intelligence so far beyond us that we cannot even properly perceive it; that is the considered view of various witnesses whose stories I trust. Another possibility is that the descriptions are real and something was seen, but that its cause was more terrestrial than extraterrestrial.

It is worth noting that, just as at Kecksburg in 1965 (see page 104), there were many odd reports of strange 'comets' and 'fireballs' in the sky that night. There was even the re-entry of a Cosmos satellite. Moreover, the site of the crash is conve-nient, for Woodbridge housed the 'Aerospace Rescue and Recovery' squadron – trained to retrieve space debris and not unlike the unit that responded at Kecksburg.

I was contacted by a senior MoD space physicist (whose credentials were *bona fide*). He had read my work and said that his investigations revealed distortions in the re-entry orbit of the Soviet satellite. Interestingly, later checks with the British Astronomical Association showed that their records illustrate a problem here too. The scientist proposed that a nuclear motor may have been purposely guided down into the forest, somehow, and then retrieved in secret. He ended by telling me it was far too sensitive an issue to research further and that his life would be in danger if he did so. I never heard from him again. Of course, it is difficult to imagine how a satellite, shot from the sky or not, could possibly be mistaken by so many trained air force personnel. It seems hard to square this idea with the facts.

Another option was leaked to Ray Boeche in 1992 by two individuals professing to be US government agents who knew the truth about the Rendlesham Forest case. They stated that their consciences were forcing them to break the massive cover-up. According to their version, the encounters were set up by top-secret defence intelligence agencies and the witnesses were innocent guinea-pigs simply describing what they saw. However, their minds had been scrambled as part of a 'psychotronic warfare' test which utilized secret electronic equipment to generate paranormal energy fields which triggered physical and psychological effects among the men.

Of course, alternative and more mundane solutions offer themselves along the lines of some kind of military accident or experiment. However, there have been debates in the British parliament and letters from senior politicians, including Michael Heseltine and Lord Trefgarne, who have both put in writing, on behalf of the government, that there has been no cover-up of such things. Of course, they may simply not have known the truth, but both held very senior posts in the MoD and presumably should be taken at their word. I also feel sure the senior witnesses involved did not know what they were watching. Assuming the sceptics' version is rejected, that leaves little option but to regard this case as a series of complex UFO encounters.

In the USA, Ray Boeche persuaded Nebraska senator James Exon to spend several months probing the data. Halt agreed to talk to him and intimated to Boeche that he could help Exon to be directed towards more physical evidence, for example, soil samples and perhaps even film that was taken. Exon took to the task reluctantly, but soon became ensnared. His staff told Boeche that they were surprised that he handled it all himself, not allowing any of them to make enquiries for him, as was usual practice. In the end, Exon told Boeche that he had spent more time on his investigation 'than any other case since I have been a US senator'. However, he refused to discuss his findings, save to note that 'additional information on the subject of the Bentwaters and other unexplained UFO incidents may exist', but that he had seen no evidence of 'a cover-up of UFO incidents'.

It seems logical that no US senator is going to devote months of his busy schedule to something so contentious; nor that he would spend more time on it than any other issue . . . At least, not unless this extraordinary case hides something pretty important behind the ever-growing facts we know.

1984:
FALLS OF MOON DUST

One of the most interesting discoveries to emerge under the FoI Act documents concerns 'Project Moon Dust'. Nothing had been known about this operation beforehand, but released files show it to be involved with the retrieval of material from space. Several such episodes have been noted in South and Central America, and it may have been the Ubatuba affair that prompted this unit to form. On the other hand, it seems to have had a special function connected with seeking out the recovery of material from earth satellites and space rocket crashes.

One Moon Dust file describes an incident in La Paz, Bolivia, on 21 August 1979. A whistling sound preceded a fireball and then an explosion in the suburb of Buen Retiro. Two spheres of metal, 'similar to copper, kind of dark with light spots', were recovered. They showed signs of having passed through the atmosphere, but they left no impact crater, almost as if they had landed smoothly. Although each was about 1 m (3 ft) in diameter, they were so light (1.4 kg/3 lb) that they could be carried away easily. Each had a hole about 23 cm (9 in) in diameter.

The data on the findings were sent to Project Moon Dust, which was apparently based at Wright Patterson air base, alongside the old UFO project headquarters and, according to testimony, various retrieved UFOs. Film taken by the Bolivian Air Force was also sent there. A Bolivian colonel spoke of how the objects were made of a specially resistant alloy that seemed designed for spaceflight, but nobody had any idea what the things were.

So far as I am aware, no follow-up data about this discovery have ever been traced, although there are other references to 'Moon Dust' in archive papers. There are grounds to suppose that this operation still exists and one can only speculate about its role in UFO-retrieval cases, such as the team sent to Kecksburg and the NASA-trained 'rescue and recovery squadron' operating out of Woodbridge air force base in Suffolk, England.

Another probable Moon Dust investigation involved Puerto Rico, an island rich in UFO encounters. It apparently occurred on 19 February 1984 in the mountains of El Yunque and it has similarities with the Kecksburg, Rendlesham and Llandrillo affairs. Knowing now about Moon Dust's use of aircraft and satellites to monitor sites where incidents occurred, one can imagine just how this case was followed up.

Jorge Martin, an experienced investigator on Puerto Rico, tracked down several witnesses. Reports did make the local Press at the time. The object in the sky was seen by many on the eastern side of the mountains as it flew across. It was said to be a round white mass with an orange border, that changed direction several times, appeared to try to climb, but then crashed into the mountains near Coca Falls. Luis Morales, a policeman at Rio Grande, says that he drove into the crash site after witnessing the incident and his car engine lost power as he approached, then stopped dead.

A major search operation was undertaken and the area was closed off for a time. The police were instructed to tell callers that the object was a meteorite, but that investigation had revealed that it had not struck the mountains after all but fallen into the sea. However, Martin spoke with air-sea rescue member Benjamin Gascot, who was puzzled by the way his team had been left out of the operation. Gascot also saw a mysterious, black, unmarked Chinook helicopter land at the air base that morning, packed with both military personnel and civilians. They were kept isolated from the experienced air-sea rescue crew and conducted their own search operation.

Another source on the air base spoke of three weeks of military presence in the area following the UFO (clearly an over-reaction for a meteorite that fell into the sea). He claimed that an intelligence officer involved in the recovery had said that radioactive debris had been recovered.

Martin also found someone at the base who saw bits of debris being packed into wooden crates, which were sprayed with a metallic substance. Mention was also made of a NASA aircraft in the area. Given that NASA is a civilian operation, this could suggest that the incident involved a NASA launching that malfunctioned, perhaps a rocket carrying a military payload. If so then it was evidently a secret operation.

1986:
A METEORITE FALLS ON THE USSR

Shortly before the USSR collapsed, a case with many similarities to Kecksburg, Llandrillo and Coca Falls seems to have occurred. Partly because of the paucity of information provided by the Communist regime, but mostly because of its remote location, we know little about it. Perhaps with the new freedom sweeping the former states of the USSR, more will come to light in future.

Early in 1986, possibly in April, an object described as a sphere of light, was seen crossing the Pacific region north of the port of Vladivostok. Superficially, it resembled a meteorite as it plunged to earth, making a terrific noise as it did so.

Many in and around the Primorskiy Kray peninsula saw its flight. This region is a rocky area that looks out towards Japan. It is also near the location where, three years earlier, a Korean Airlines jumbo jet had been shot down by a Soviet pilot who thought it was on a spying mission. Clearly this is not an area where aerial intruders would simply be ignored.

Villagers at Dalnegorsk heard an explosion and plotted the impact point to the side of a mountain known as Hill 611. Trees were set on fire and the area was devastated. The object disintegrated upon impact.

Scientists from the Moscow Academy of Sciences visited the area and found peculiar pieces of metal and the same kind of glassy balls that were at the other two Russian crash sites earlier in the century. Metal analysis suggested an unidentified type of chromium was present.

To date, no one is sure what the object was. There are, of course, those who think that it may have been a spacecraft. A few still favour the meteorite theory. However, quite a strong strand of opinion seems to suggest that it was a globule of plasma energy that detonated on impact with the ground and fused the local rocks. This idea owes something to the UFO theory about quartz crystals in rocks generating floating, ionized plasmas at rocky zones around the world. These window areas are well established and Primorskiy Kray seems a perfect example, with lights in the sky having been seen on many previous occasions. But explosive detonations such as this are not known at other UFO windows, although unexplained bangs have been heard at sites, for example, at Todmorden in the Pennines in Britain.

1989:
UFO DOWNED BY LASER OVER SOUTH AFRICA

Quite the most dramatic report yet of a UFO crash surfaced in 1990 with the claim that the South African Air Force had actually shot one out of the sky, and then successfully covered up the incident.

Tony Dodd, a former police officer who has seen over 60 UFOs in the Pennines, is a co-ordinator of Quest, formerly the Yorkshire UFO Society. It takes a very strong stand on UFOs, believing them to be extraterrestrial in origin. Consequently, it attracts much support from many like-minded UFO enthusiasts. However, it remains rather aloof from Britain's other main UFO group, BUFORA, which professes itself to be objective and scientific in its analysis of evidence, often from non-ET perspectives. Poles apart, the groups rarely see eye to eye and they tend to steer clear of each other.

Dodd claims that, in July 1989, he was contacted by a man whose identity remained secret for some time, but who later emerged as Captain James van Greunen, a special investigations intelligence officer with the South African Air Force. According to van Greunen, a UFO had been downed in the Kalahari Desert, on the border between South Africa and Botswana. The two jets involved were Mirage fighters out of Valhalla air base and they were each armed with an experimental laser cannon, which obviously proved its worth. Moreover van Greunen could prove his case with documentation. This duly arrived at Dodd's house in the form of a small typed dossier rather like the one APEN had sent to me on the 1974 Llandrillo crash (see page 112). It appeared without any return address. The file was very dramatic and gave a story rich in detail. At 1.45 pm on 7 May 1989, a naval vessel claimed to have detected a UFO on its radar and set Cape Town on full alert. Seven minutes later, the UFO, travelling at almost 9,600 km/h (6,000 mph), entered South African air space. By now, it had been picked up by various radar stations, including America's NORAD system. Mirages were scrambled, but they failed to establish contact, so the squadron-leader in charge was ordered to attack the UFO with a 'Thor' laser cannon. The UFO was hit, bright flashes emerged from it, and it began to waver. Just after 2 pm, it crashed into the desert. A team of intelligence officers and medical personnel were immediately sent to the spot, while the Mirage jets circled above, keeping watch until the retrieval operation had been concluded.

At the location, according to the file, there was a huge crater with a silvery disc more or less intact, embedded in it at an angle. The sand had fused with the heat of the impact and there were strong radiation and other energy readings around the craft. The recovery of the UFO was an apparently smooth operation. Back at the air base, things really livened up. A loud noise was followed by a hatch opening, out of which stepped two living extraterrestrials!

The aliens were promptly shipped to a medical unit for examination. They were said to be just over 120 cm (4 ft) tall, with grey skins, no body hair, over-large heads and huge, slanted eyes. They were very aggressive and scratched the face of one of the doctors! No communication was made with them, according to the report. Reputedly, the two entities were to be sent, with their craft, to Wright Patterson for a more detailed study by the US government.

Of course, this is a fantastic story, but it begs a number of questions. In particular, one wonders why the South African government turned over such an amazing prize so easily to one of the countries actively involved in bringing down that government.

When the documents began to circulate among the UFO movement (followed later by a photograph that purported to show a third dead occupant), there was much controversy. Tim Good (a staunch supporter of alien UFOs and a firm believer in the Roswell crash) cautioned against taking more anonymous documents to heart. Given the then simmering MJ–12 debate (see page 129), which he had partly precipitated, this was probably very sensible. Then van Greunen allegedly turned up in Britain and Dodd grilled the intelligence officer in depth about the case before he left, ostensibly for Wright Patterson to join in the investigation.

Van Greunen was willing to risk what he claimed was a treasonable offence in South Africa, because to tell the world about this affair could not be considered an act of treason against humankind. However, when Dodd checked out his intelligence credentials, van Greunen's activities became known in Pretoria and he was ordered home. Later, he fled South Africa to Germany, where early versions of the story first appeared in the Press.

Respected American UFO writer Antonio Huneeus reports that when he quizzed Dodd about this case in autumn 1989, new details emerged. It seems that there had been hieroglyphics inside the UFO and a symbol on the outside. The symbol was an arch with an upward-pointing arrow inside, exactly the same as the sign seen on the side of a well-reported and authentic-sounding UFO which landed in Socorro, New Mexico, in April 1964. In addition, Huneeus learnt that the laser cannon was a 'maser', which used beams of microwave energy.

The UFO community in Britain was split between those excited by these dramatic revelations and amazed that the story had not been given greater prominence in the media and others who seemed bent on trying to discredit the whole episode.

UFO Brigantia published a typically destructive analytical commentary in May 1990. It left no doubt about its opinion of the case. Using sources in South Africa who lived near the site, it claimed to have found that there were no known witnesses and no evidence that the area was sealed off or that trucks carrying a UFO had been seen. Another problem was that the secret document was in English, not Afrikaans (the language used by the South African Air Force), and that the term squadron-leader is not even used as a rank there. This and other factors caused the documentation to be called into serious question. Overall, it felt that the story left a lot to be desired. Quest, too, now seemed more cautious about it, while still looking objectively into the details it reported.

According to *Brigantia*, various sources in South Africa were now alleging that the government had arranged a swap with American President Bush: two nuclear bombs for the spaceship! It seems inconceivable that such a plan would ever be considered, let alone implemented, especially, as *Brigantia* succinctly pointed out, since the US seems to have more than enough crashed UFOs of its own, so why claim one more? The case descended into controversy. You could either believe the sources that Quest had found and, clearly quite honestly, had trusted and promoted, or accept *Brigantia*'s cynical appraisal of the matter. Then, in May 1993, Cynthia Hind entered the fray and produced what seems (at least to date) to be the definitive word on the topic.

Cynthia is Africa's top ufologist, a member of the American group MUFON and a believer in the extraterrestrial hypothesis. She is also a good investigator. She lives in Zimbabwe and has a network of contacts throughout the continent which includes David Powell, Prier Wintle and Nathan Middledorf. Cynthia found the evidence seriously wanting. Van Greunen was a UFO buff, an avid reader of books and a MUFON member by the age of 16. The anonymous documents about the crash began to look more and more suspect, with much of the data not fitting accepted practices. The UFO's 'hieroglyphics', said to be the 'Crem alphabet' from 'Reticuli', were checked at Johannesburg University and found to be completely unacceptable to them as a language. In other instances where such messages had been published, they had at least been plausible, even if hoaxes.

One by one, those who had been impressed began to draw back. Van Greunen disappeared from his new home in Germany, just as the questions toughened up. His girlfriend said that the poor agent had been 'executed' by the South Africans, without providing any evidence to back up her claim. Indeed, Cynthia reports that he has been sighted in Cairo since then.

This is one story that may continue to run and run. We have no way of knowing the truth, or whether van Greunen believed what he was reporting. Nonetheless, as evidence of a UFO crash, it cannot be taken seriously.

CHAPTER EIGHT

THE SHOW GOES ON

You might think that all these stories are fine in their place –
the past. However, in the 1990s, these claims cannot possibly be
made with much hope of justification.

Think again. They can – and do – crop up from time to time,
pretty much as before. Of course, the good news is that we have
now developed a degree of sophistication in handling them. As
the South African 'laser cannon' affair showed, a crash
retrieval now, has to be followed up in painstaking detail before
most ufologists will stand behind it. That is very much
for the better.

However, something else has changed – technology. As you will
see, the camcorder has suddenly come into its own and offers a
whole new dimension for us to explore. Given their widespread
use, a retrieval would eventually be captured by a prying lens.

And, indeed, one has. It will be discussed next and you must
make up your own mind about its credibility. However, if
spaceships really are falling out of the skies with anything like
the alarming frequency that stories in this book imply, then it
will not be the only case for very long.

There are now dozens of camcorder films reputedly showing
UFOs in the sky. In 1988, British ufologists investigated the first
case where an alleged spacenap victim photographed the alien
that reputedly abducted him. Now we have video of a UFO
retrieval under way. How long before we have full-colour, take-
it-or-leave-it film of one of the archetypal aliens performing for
the camera? Now that would be something worth waiting for.

1991:
GUARDIAN OF THE TRUTH?

In the rich farmland west of Ottawa, in August 1991, a drama
was said to have occurred that has set the UFO world buzzing.

155

But is the story true or just another tall tale?

Like many of the cases we have discussed in this book, it had an unpromising start. I first heard about it in mid-1993 from Maria Ward, a UFO witness-cum-researcher, who had submitted the evidence to a TV programme, *The Magic and Mystery Show*, in which I was involved with Eammon Holmes, who is also interested in UFOs. He was as keen as I to learn more about this matter and, during a break in rehearsals at the Ipswich location, suggested I talked to Maria. She explained to me that the case had come directly to an American, Bob Oeschler, from an anonymous source whom he had known since 1989. I had never met Oeschler, but I was aware of his status in the UFO field as a controversial ex-NASA researcher who featured in many of the stories of cover-up and conspiracy. At this stage I had seen only part of the evidence, but Maria had more to offer. Later I came to see further examples and study Oeschler's own account of what had taken place. Like Eammon Holmes, I remained intrigued, but I was also aware of the possibility that Oeschler may have been set up. Once you face possible disinformation, as I had done in the Rendlesham Forest affair, the spectre of that option is never far from your mind.

The story began in late 1989, when Oeschler's source, who called himself 'Guardian', claimed that the area west of Ottawa, which had been rife in sightings, had produced a remarkable incident on 4 November 1989. An object was tracked on radar over Carp before it fell in a sudden plunge towards the ground, crashing into swamps near West Carleton. The area was immediately sealed off and huge helicopters and military units, specially trained to deal with UFO retrievals, were flown in. They even used satellites to track the progress of the aliens who had escaped!

Guardian was also in contact with other ufologists in Canada and the USA and he offered a fantastic amount of details about what was going on. According to him, the alien craft used a pulsing electromagnetic field to fly and was built from a 'matrixed-dielectric magnesium alloy'. It also generated cold fusion radiation (cold fusion, of course, being the 'in' thing at that time). Reputedly, the alien mission had a malevolent purpose: to set East against West during the final days of Communism in the old Soviet Empire. It was the forerunner of an interstellar invasion. Three entities, with heads like the foetus of a reptile, were eventually recovered from the area.

They were descendants of the dinosaurs which had fled into space over 60 million years ago, allowing primitive mammals to evolve into humans. Now they were back to reclaim their planet. Frankly, this might make a good science-fiction movie, but it barely seemed credible, even to UFO researchers used to dealing with fantastic scenarios. However, the story was far from over. It was only just beginning.

In February 1992 Oeschler claims that a package arrived at his home near Washington. It was postmarked Ottawa, had no sender's address (as usual), but contained the code-name 'Guardian' and a fingerprint on the top for 'identification'. Inside the package, there was a video tape and several documents, including a map of the area around Carp and West Carleton. The documents did not refer to the 1989 crash but to another, even more extraordinary, event that had taken place on 18 August 1991.

The documents, according to Oeschler, were 'fabricated' with official Canadian defence markings and had had data deleted by a thick, black pen. The material rambled on about religion, the Apocalypse and the ancient prophecies of Nostradamus, medieval astrologer and doom merchant. Indeed, Oeschler himself adds that, without the accompanying video, few would have paid much heed to the other material. In fact, he consulted psychologists about the contents of Guardian's package and they claimed to see evidence of a kind of pathological obsession within it, as shown by his interpretation of the supposed intergalactic goings on. However, Oeschler regarded these 'commentaries' as secondary to the hard evidence found on the video tape, which he called 'exceptional'.

The tape was analysed in detail during the spring of 1992 and Oeschler claims that it showed evidence of having been 'edited' – a series of short snatches of image was all that remained from a scene that was evidently much longer. The tape runs for over 30 minutes, although only the first six minutes show moving images; the remainder comprises freeze-frame stills, including some of scenes that are not on the moving footage. These include the most remarkable imagery of all: close-ups of a purported alien being's face! The fact that none of these shots is in motion – although there are sequences of stills that appear to suggest motion had occurred between shots – is probably the most negative aspect of this case. These are the very images that would be near impossible to hoax, if shown as full video; yet, despite offering good, moving clarity for the scenes without aliens in them, the ones with the alien face are muted.

All of the film was shot at night and appears to show a rotating disc-like craft with a dome on top and a series of bright lights, including a pulsating light at the apex. Some blue and red as well as white is visible, and in some sequences the tree line in the background is illuminated. What appear to be flares shine from time to time. Throughout this whole scenario, the camera operator is walking towards the UFO with a hand-held camcorder, so the video is jerky.

Certainly, the images look spectacular, particularly when the UFO fills much of the screen on zoom setting. However, sight of anything more than the bright lights, and occasional dim outlines of a shape behind them, is missing. After initial enthusiasm about this video being 'the one', realization dawns. Yes, it might be a large craft far from the camera, but it is difficult, if not impossible, to be sure that this is not a much smaller model considerably closer than that and with some trees in the background. The nocturnal definition – despite, as Oeschler says from tests he carried out, this being an expensive, professional field camera – is still such that nothing is really certain. Oeschler seems satisfied that the UFO is not a model and that a retrieval of some sort was filmed and evidence then sneaked out.

As for the entity, curiously, no full figure is ever visible. Instead head and hands stand out in a luminosity, while the rest of the torso is invisible. There is no sign of ambient illumination, which implies that the entity is 'glowing', something that few accounts from UFO witnesses have ever mentioned. Oeschler notes that it would be possible to fake these images fairly easily with a mask and a black suit that absorbed light from the rest of the body. In truth, little more than two large, black, slanted eyes on a pasty white face are ever visible. However, Oeschler claims that it would be illogical to assume that the still images of the alien would be a hoax if the UFO film is genuine. Since he believes the UFO footage to be real, so, presumably, are the stills of the alien face.

I would not go along with that reasoning myself. If, for instance, someone filmed a military exercise, where there were flares and a hovering, well-lit helicopter, and the carefully edited film resembled a UFO, then tacking on a few stills of a child in a suit and some sort of mask would hardly be beyond the skills of most people.

Of course, this is all pure surmise. The UFO might be as much of a fake as the alien, or, just conceivably, Oeschler is correct and both are genuine. If so, we can only curse the fact that Guardian's source (assuming he did not take the film himself) failed to get any moving images of the recovered alien, for reasons that seem difficult to imagine. Clearly, the camcorder was working properly and it was taken very close to the alleged alien, so it makes little sense not to have videoed the entity.

To be fair, Bob Oeschler says that he set out to visit the site in Canada in May 1992 only satisfied that the video was 'potentially authentic', which is a reasonable attitude to adopt. He spent several days in the Carp–West Carleton area with investigators from CUFORN (Canadian UFO Research Network), a respected group. They spoke with a woman called Labenek, who had been a witness to the 1989 sighting. She reluctantly indicated that other things had happened in this remote area since then. They traced a circular area nearby, about 15 m (50 ft) wide, where the plants were bleached and there was evidence that the ground had been affected by microwave radiation. Samples were taken and a black powder on the leaves was found to be titanium, a most unusual finding.

Armed with this discovery, they returned to Mrs Labenek. The investigators also told her about the Guardian's video tape for the first time. Mrs Labenek now told them about something she had witnessed the previous August. After putting her children to bed, she claimed to have seen red fires through the big picture window on the first floor. She thought about contacting the fire service, but decided not to. Her children watched the same scene from their bedroom, as did their neighbour, Dr Quarrington, from his house. They all saw a white disc fall towards the trees and into the area where the red fires (now suggested as flares) were situated. They observed a pyrotechnic display similar to the one on the video, but saw no aliens.

However, another local woman claimed that she had. She had been alerted by her barking dog. On going to investigate, she saw the lights in the trees. At closer range, she saw the inside of the craft and two small beings with yellowy-white skins and oriental features. One of them looked ill and was moving in slow motion. She then lost consciousness and recovered back inside her house, with the sound of a helicopter swooping low over the area.

The speculation appears to be that this 1991 encounter may have been an attempted rescue mission for the UFO that had crashed two years earlier!

In August 1993 I spoke to a Canadian researcher visiting Britain and asked for his comments on the case. He told both Paul Fuller and me that he had visited the area in question, looking for proof that this startling case was real, but he found no physical evidence on the ground and no eyewitnesses willing to state that they had observed the episode. However, a couple of local farmers did apparently remember a 'military exercise' in the area.

On the other hand, according to Oeschler, the video has been subjected to considerable analysis during 1992. Dr Robert Nathan, at NASA's Jet Propulsion Laboratory in Pasadena, California, could not find evidence of trickery. TV company NBC were given the film and, he says, spent up to a quarter of a million dollars in their attempt to recreate it in early 1993, but they failed to do so to Oeschler's satisfaction.

Sightings, apparently, continue to be reported in this wooded area and this story seems to be set for a long life. However, mainstream ufology, even in the USA, has been slow to embrace it in the way it did previous 'big' cases, such as the incessantly debated 'Gulf Breeze' still photos from 1987.

1994:
THE LATEST RETRIEVAL

In April 1994 I got a call from Sky Television in the UK, a network which seems particularly fascinated by UFOs (perhaps not surprisingly given their name). What did I know about Britain's UFO crash, I was asked? The answer was straightforward: unless they were referring to any of the cases mentioned earlier in this book, absolutely nothing. I soon learnt that it was not an old case that Sky was asking me about, but a crash 'within the past six months somewhere north of Birmingham', which was all they knew.

I made some enquiries and was interested to learn that Nick Pope, then head of the MoD section, 'Air Staff 2A', which handles UFO data, had heard the story as well. He seemed to know no more than I did about its status or details, but it showed how times had changed when an MoD official did not hide things and was as keen as anyone to see if there was any-thing behind the rumour.

Eventually, the breaking of the story was traced back to Quest, the Yorkshire UFO group which was the first to hear of the South African affair mentioned earlier. Or, at least, it had been one of the earliest known points of reference for the new story, having picked it up from their contacts.

I include this incident in the book because it illustrates how crash-retrieval cases begin as a whisper and end in one of two ways: either growing into a roar, signifying perhaps truth or bravado, or else fading into subliminal echoes that are even-tually never heard of again. More often than not, these tales commence as rumours and for a long time remain only as 'an unknown source told so-and-so that . . .'. In the end, a named source might appear to back up or expand upon what is known and, if we are lucky (or not), the snowball grows ever bigger as it rolls down the hill.

So, for what it is worth, here is what I have picked up from reliable (and not so reliable) 'moles' and contacts so far. In late November or early December 1993, a bright light was seen to cross the skies of eastern England. It came down – possibly forced down, but not shot down, by military jets – somewhere in an isolated part of Cleveland, north of the Yorkshire moors and not too far from the old Fylingdales early warning radar station.

The UFO was shaped like a tube and not very large, per-haps twice the size of a car. It was embedded in wet earth and stuck firm. A convoy of military vehicles arrived and secured the area, which was quiet because it was late at night. However, it was obvious that it would be impossible to remove the object before any locals or the media heard about the mat-ter. This was not Arizona, where a reporter would have had to drive for hours to reach the site: TV cameras could have been there inside minutes. Thus another plan was adopted.

It was decided to cover the UFO with earth so that it would look like a slag heap, albeit a curiously placed one in the middle of a field. Then, with the time gained, a temporary shelter or building would be constructed around it. I am less than clear whether this was intended to be a short-term or per-manent arrangement, although one source did tell me that the UFO was still buried there and being studied *in situ*. However, now that the 'cover' was blown, this would be quickly rectified and the spaceship relocated somewhere. Wright Patterson in

Ohio has yet to be suggested, but I guess it is only a matter of time before it is. Time will certainly tell if this is the nonsense that it certainly seems to be. British people are pretty unobservant but would the residents of Cleveland really not notice such mysterious goings-on all around them?

I did some checking and discovered that in mid- to late November there were a number of genuine UFO sightings in the York and Scarborough area which might fit this possible scenario. An object, resembling a 'comet' with a tail, was seen to glide through the sky from the North Sea. I had written the case off as a meteor sighting, but then funny meteors have cropped up in these retrieval stories before. On 9 December there was a major sighting on the east coast around Louth, south of the Humber estuary. So many witnesses saw the object pass overhead that there is little doubt that something odd was flying about. The MoD have confirmed to me that it received a report from a senior officer at the RAF base at Donna Nook, which is used as a practice bombing range on the east coast. The base had no aircraft in the air then, but it received reports from the public and one of its commanders saw the object. He could not identify it but said it looked like an unusual and well-lit triangular aircraft.

According to an investigation into the Louth case, villagers in and around Fulstowe also reported unusual electrical interference affecting lights and TVs that night. Whether this was connected with the UFO is hard to say.

The Louth–Donna Nook affair was probably the most important British UFO sighting of 1993 and the MoD was willing to put in writing to me that it did not have an explanation for it. I have been to the Lincolnshire coast myself to make a film for the US TV series *Sightings*, and I was very impressed with the quality of the evidence. Of course, neither of these incidents may be relevant to the alleged UFO crash; unless, or until, we get more information it is impossible to tell. Perhaps there is more to this latest story that we do not yet know, or perhaps this will prove to be another piece of garbled disinformation. Then again, it may just be another hoax fed into the UFO community by an unknown outside source for reasons best known to itself. Consequently, Britain's new sensation may end with a bang or a whimper and right now I would not like to hazard a guess as to which.

CHAPTER NINE

CONCLUSIONS: THE TRUTH BEHIND RETRIEVALS

You have just read a series of extraordinary case histories, some of them, of course, hoaxes – some simple, others complicated. A complex web of deception has been spun by a variety of individuals – from story-tellers keen to appear on TV, people wanting to tread the boards of the lucrative US lecture circuit, to shady intelligence agents intent on spreading disinformation.

In some instances, however, it is likely that there really was a crash and, indeed sometimes, that there was an attempted retrieval of whatever came down. Incidents such as Tunguska, Roswell, Kecksburg, Llandrillo and Rendlesham Forest leave little alternative. But, of course, that is not the same thing as stating that the objects which crashed were extraterrestrial spaceships.

Other options that need to be taken into account have been frequently cited – from meteor falls to secret V-rocket missions, and from experimental aircraft to nuclear motors falling off man-made satellites. In one way or another, perhaps, these things will unite to provide the answers to all of the mysteries which we have just confronted.

However, it would be foolish to rule out the possibility that something earth-shattering lurks behind a small handful of these episodes. I doubt that more than half a dozen of the cases analysed stand up even as potential candidates for bonafide alien retrievals. But, of course, it needs only one to be established as fact for the universe to change. The discovery that we are not alone in the vastness of space – that we have been visited, possibly for centuries, by superior beings from another world – would alter our conception of our place within the cosmos; it is impossible to oversell its importance. That is why – ridiculous as the idea of alien crash/retrievals may appear to most rational people, and rightly so – we have to overcome our prejudice and look at the evidence with an open mind.

I have tried to be even-handed, to let you judge the facts. I certainly have no need to prove that these cases are real, or unreal. It would affect my belief in UFOs not one jot if every single crash were explained in non-alien terms; that is because I know that 95 per cent of all sightings are misperceptions of other things and most (if not all) of the unresolved cases relate to natural phenomena of various types that science has yet to fully comprehend. This I believe is an incontrovertible fact that stares you in the face when you do any serious investigation of the evidence. Conceivably, no UFOs are alien in origin.

On the other hand, as an earlier book of mine (*Looking for the Aliens*) firmly establishes, the idea of aliens visiting our world is far from being a logical absurdity: it is a legitimate branch of scientific enquiry to which many leading astronomical experts should at least pay heed. Equally, there remain enough riddles within the UFO data itself to make it foolhardy to conclude that no case ever was the product of alien contact. Of course, accepting this as a possibility is very different from asserting that it is proven. In no sense would I attempt to suggest we know the truth, although some of my more vociferous colleagues would – and, indeed, do – do so with quite alarming degrees of apparent assurance.

In other words, if any of these cases does truly hide an alien retrieval, it is not something that would challenge my basic preconceptions: I accept it is possible. I believe it might represent the best answer in one or two of the events described, and that is as far as it is safe to go on the strength of the present evidence. The rest is down to value judgement and personal assessment. But at least you are now as capable of making that sort of decision as anyone, including myself. Of course, which road you choose to take may still be coloured by your own expectations about what is – or, rather, is not – considered acceptable to science.

However, on the premise (which I consider reasonable) that at least one of these stories may well describe a real alien retrieval, it is appropriate to end on a series of questions that must arise from that startling possibility.

WHAT DO WE KNOW ABOUT THE CRAFT ITSELF?

We have seen frequent references to an unusually light, highly durable metal which reputedly has no equivalent on earth. It is used to create what is almost always a disc-like craft, although conical or tubular objects have been reported too. The size of the craft varies from not much bigger than a small car to the dimensions of a moderate aircraft; rarely is anything bigger than that hinted at by the evidence.

The propulsion system is often described as incomprehensible. However, some stories suggest a twin method – one for use outside the atmosphere; the other for use once within our environment. That might imply that a strongly irradiating source propels the vehicle through space, but that a different method is required where serious contamination might be left behind – an interesting line of thought which one would not expect to find in a bunch of unrelated myths and rumours. Indeed, the atmospheric flight system is said to have characteristics of a strong pulsing magnetic field which can leave its mark – for example, stalling car engines, and radio and TV interference. Ionization of the air, causing it to glow, is another frequent reference to what may be a side-effect of the propulsion system.

Certainly, this technology – which, if real, is clearly beyond our means today – would be the real prize for any government that retrieved a crashed UFO. From everything that I have learnt in my research, this would be the overriding reason for any cover-up, not the cliché of mass panic or people fleeing into the streets, screaming 'the aliens have landed'. The story – if told – would be news for a few days but, since there would be no sign of an alien invasion or threat to individual lives, would quickly fade from the scene to be replaced by items of more direct relevance.

The prize of the secrets of alien technology would be enormous. I was told by a senior figure in Britain's Defence Ministry that finding out how UFOs do what they do is purpose number one behind any study of the data; as it was phrased, 'We have to learn to use this to build weapons before the other side do.' This same factor seems critical, from what little we know, to the thinking of security agencies, such as the CIA and, probably, the NSA, which delve into UFO reports.

WHAT ARE THE ALIENS SAID TO BE LIKE?

Anything up to 20 alien bodies have reputedly been captured from crashes since 1947; indeed, in one or two cases, it is claimed that the aliens were alive, at least upon initial recovery. The descriptions of these beings is far more consistent than anything else within the data. In fact, they are so consistent they represent either a startling reality underlying these cases or some kind of conspirational fakery.

From at least 1950, there are references to the body size being small – between about 1 and 1.25 m (3 and 4 ft) being the norm. There are common references to the heads being disproportionately large and the eyes being unusual, typically being described as large, slanted or oriental in appearance and dark in colour.

The other attributes of the body are less well recorded, with nose, ears and mouths being undeveloped or not noticed by casual observers. However, the body is said to be sleek, almost oddly super-light in appearance, even fragile. Not uncommonly, the hands only have four (lightly webbed) digits, not five. Skin tone is often said to be white, grey or bluish in

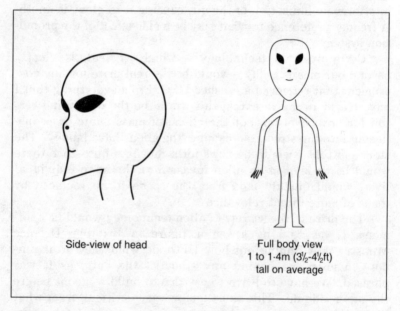

Side-view of head

Full body view
1 to 1·4m (3½-4½ft)
tall on average

A montage, compiled from alleged eyewitness accounts, depicting a captured alien body.

colour, although not consistently.

Most of these accounts come from brief observations by witnesses said to be at the site of a crash, and viewing the bodies without permission, or at Wright Patterson after their arrival, where a snatched glimpse is all that is possible. However, there are a few cases of alleged autopsy reports, for example, like those leaked to Len Stringfield by doctors. When Peter Hough and I were offered the MJ–12 files (complete with appendices) by our military source, one of the key features, described to us at length, was a very detailed autopsy report allegedly performed by one Dr Frederick Hauser.

The military source had read Dr Hauser's 200-page autopsy of an entity (photographs of which he claimed were included) and he said the entity was 'eerily human-like'. It was 'smaller than average size and completely bald, with no eyebrows or eyelashes. No body hair at all. The nose was the most unusual feature, very flush into the face, almost not there . . . The text was full of incredible medical jargon, most of it right over my head.' He added that there was an incision 'right down the middle of the body.' But he did not know if this was because of the autopsy.

Stringfield's data from an 'anatomical study', allegedly from the early 1950s, were very specific: the entity's height was given as 'four feet three and three-eighth inches'! It added: 'The head was pear-shaped in appearance and oversized by human standards . . . The eyes were Mongoloid . . . The eyes were recessed into the head. There seemed to be no visible eyelids . . . The skin seemed greyish in colour and seemed mobile when moved'. There was much more to it than this.

However, possibly the most startling description of the entities comes from Dr Robert Sarbacher. Before his death in 1986 (a year, incidentally, in which a large number of key figures in the crash-retrieval story, from Allen Hynek to Jesse Marcel, were lost to us), this scientist issued what may be the most important on-the-record statement on the matter.

Sarbacher was a brilliant man, as his entry in *Who's Who* clearly shows. He was consultant to the American government's research and development board and later chairman of the prestigious Washington Institute of Technology. As early as 1950 he told a top Canadian scientist, Dr Wilbert Smith, in a private meeting, that UFOs were 'the most highly classified subject in the US government', beating even the H-bomb by two points. Moreover, that by three years after the first sightings 'we have not been able to duplicate their performance', but he could not elaborate on any of the research going on.

Smith revealed this information and Sarbacher had then clammed up, but in the last three years of his life he decided to put the record straight, apparently fearing nobody. Several times, verbally and in writing, he mentioned the top scientific and military team assigned to retrievals in the 1950s, how he missed out on much of the action due to other commitments, but how he learnt of the UFO and alien technology that was recovered. The UFO materials were 'extremely light and very tough', he noted, affirming in 1983 what many first-hand sources have said. As for the entities, they too were 'very light-weight' and, indeed, 'I got the impression these "aliens" were constructed like certain insects we have observed on earth, wherein, because of the low mass, the inertial forces involved would be quite low.' If all of these stories were fantasies, then they are amazingly consistent.

WHERE WOULD THEY KEEP CAPTURED SPACESHIPS?

Again and again we hear reference to captured wreckage being shipped to Wright Patterson air force base in Dayton, Ohio. In most cases this is based upon testimony, either of people at the site who saw the debris despatched, or people at Wright Patterson itself, who saw the stuff *in situ* or as it arrived. However, in the Roswell case, we know from the written records of the time that this is exactly where the recovered wreckage was shipped.

Wright Patterson is an obvious choice. It houses the Foreign Technology Division, which assesses hardware cap-tured from other countries, including, no doubt, anything extraterrestrial. Indeed, there are also grounds for thinking that some of the materials from non-American incidents went there, although other countries (notably the USSR) have their own facilities.

Security is the key factor. There are many stories and rumours about a well-guarded complex, sometimes called Hangar 18, other times 'the blue room', at Wright Patterson. Senator Barry Goldwater made references to his attempts to enter what may be these premises in the mid-1960s, yet despite his then very creditable status within the government, he was seemingly denied access because of some great secret to be found there. There are stories about friends of the various presidents (for example, noted entertainer Jackie Gleason) who have confided to close relatives before their death about being let in on 'the big secret' and seeing the UFOs or alien bodies.

However, the big question is: could such a discovery be hidden for up to half a century (if Roswell was the start), apparently without anything of substance being learnt? Surely by now the greatest minds on earth would have found some way to make the technology work and there would be patents in operation as the prize won by any government that was involved? Yet that does not appear to be happening. Moreover, we are still roaring into space using 'primitive' rockets which seem to owe nothing to the sophistication of the alleged UFOs flying about our skies. Does that really make any sense?

Of course, this assumes that the technology is not centuries ahead of us, and thus so incomprehensible that we cannot fathom it out at all. Imagine Concorde crash-landing in King Arthur's court in the sixth century AD. They might have figured out that it was a flying machine, but nothing else would make any sense. This is not just because it is advanced technology: people then had no concept of electricity, computers, microchip technology, television screens, and so on – not even the basic idea about how powered flight was achievable. They simply could not have understood the principles of, let alone duplicated, Concorde.

So one can envisage some jealous government keeping alien technology under wraps, waiting for the day of scientific enlightenment to dawn, perhaps gradually understanding what they had – one small piece at a time – and incorporating this into their own advancing technology. To the outside world nothing dramatic would be happening, but that government would be virtually guaranteed an economic edge on all its rivals – a near-unlimited supply of future knowledge waiting to be chipped off bit by bit and ensuring that this nation maintained a lead in many technological fields.

Perhaps altruism might prevail; that the discovery of UFO material would be shared with all. Indeed, that the best hope of understanding it would be to bring in the top experts, whatever their nationality. But the truth is that all nations are motivated by economic factors and thrive on capitalistic rivalry. A retrieved UFO would convey so much of an advantage in terms of science, technology and military supremacy that it is hard to imagine a government that would sacrifice its own objectives and hand the evidence over to everyone else instead. This is particularly true if the first retrieval were made in 1947, when the world was a very different place. For the next couple of decades, we lived in constant fear of blowing up one another and the forces that dictated self-possession for any owners of vastly superior alien technology were irresistible, on the grounds of patriotism and self-preservation alone.

Things may have eased, especially if little was gleaned from UFO crashes after 20 or 30 years – perhaps that is the reason for the claimed move towards an 'education programme'. But another problem arises if you have hidden this truth for so very long: just how do you admit it without engaging the wrath of the planet for having put your own interests ahead of its?

Of course, all this is educated guesswork. However, one thing is clear: it seems improbable that anything of substance is at Wright Patterson today, assuming, of course, it ever was. Too many stories about it have leaked out and it is no longer secure enough. Instead the focal point of all attention is now somewhere utterly different and also far more sensible as the guardian of allegedly incredible secrets – a place known as 'Dreamland'.

ARE THERE EARTHLY SPACECRAFT UNDER DEVELOPMENT AT A US BASE?

The story about Dreamland had an inauspicious start in the early 1980s, thanks to the now discredited 'Project Aquarius' files. Bill Moore has admitted his role in monitoring their effect on ufologists when these files were fed out as disinformation by an intelligence source. Of course, in the game of bluff and counter-bluff, they may contain some nuggets of truth. In any case, they spoke of a project initiated in the Nevada Desert in 1972 whose aim was to build and test-fly a UFO, possibly a retrieved craft, or one built using some of its technology

Interest soon focused on Area 51, later called S-4, a remote part of the Nellis air force base complex surrounded by the Tonopah base test range. It is, virtually, in the middle of the

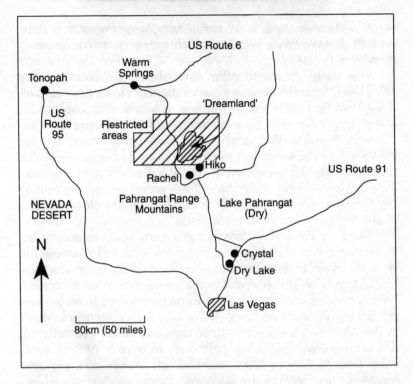

A map showing the alleged location of 'Dreamland'.

desert, near dried-out Groom Lake, several hours' drive from Las Vegas. It is subject to intense security; not that it needs it, given its relative inaccessibility. This was certainly a much more sensible home for crashed spaceships – with the best secrecy in the world you could not fly in and out of Wright Patterson without being noticed!

Once the American UFO movement got its teeth into these stories, the myth grew and grew. By 1987, sources were coming forward, alleging first-hand involvement and risking their lives by breaking the extraordinary cover-up. Dreamland, by the way, is supposedly the name given to Area 51 by its workers, because the things you can see in there are an aviation expert's equivalent of heaven.

I have seen film and photographs of the area taken by brave ufologists who have camped out on mountain tops, risking rattlesnakes, searing heat and the all-too-real threat of arrest and an instant $500 fine. They depict the intense activity that goes on there. It is, undoubtedly, the home of much secret technology and, more than likely, would be where alien spacecraft were being test-flown if this claim is anything other than pure fantasy.

One early source to offer data about this location was John Lear, from the famous aviation family. He had researched Area 51 to find out what 'spy planes' it was developing, but he allegedly got far more than he bargained for, hearing from his aviation contacts that spaceships were being flown by the USAF above the sandy bed of Groom Lake. This was about the time when the US government fought off much political pressure to close almost 36,000 ha (90,000 acres) of land surrounding the base, so that no civilian could even get close enough to see the location, let alone enter it!

Then, in 1988, along came Bob Lazar, who claimed to be an engineer and physicist who had worked at Los Alamos and been taken on various occasions (in buses with their windows blacked out) to the site at Groom Lake. Los Alamos denied having records of his employment and he claimed to be in danger for telling what he knew. Lazar has been a regular feature of the American UFO scene since then and confirmed much of the detail suspected by the believers. In March 1989 he took John Lear to Groom Lake to watch an orange disk perform incredible manoeuvres. He adds that there are nine spaceships of different designs on the base and that they use completely fantastic technology which involves, in unknown ways, the utilization of gravity waves, anti-matter and an element that cannot even be synthesized on earth.

As the tales about Dreamland continued, more sources emerged. Ufologists received documents detailing secret pacts between the aliens and the US government, exchanging UFO technology for a quota of abductee victims for medical experiments. We heard that dozens of aliens were working in Area 51, side by side with the USAF, to perfect these latest craft and that a battle was afoot between the taller 'good guys' and the small grey creatures who seemingly have little concern about humanity.

Soon it was almost impossible to separate truth from exaggeration and fact from fiction; everything claimed about Area 51 just could not be true, and, conceivably, none of it was. If so, many people were now lying.

In 1993 I met a British pilot who had been flying over the Nevada Desert on his way to California, when he had sensed, rather than seen, something in the air. He snatched his camera and took one shot of what he thought was streaking past his private jet. The picture had come out. He showed it to me: it was a black, fuzzy shape, seemingly crashing through the air at very great speed. He is adamant that, whatever it was, it created an 'aura' about it that was invisible to the naked eye, but not to film. Is this proof of advanced technology over the Groom Lake area? Perhaps. The pilot is by no means the only person to have seen or filmed things in the sky. Residents in California have also reported loud explosions, just like sonic booms, rocking their homes. But when they have looked into the sky, nothing is visible. Aviation sources believe these are top-secret aircraft on flights from Nevada which, at supersonic speeds, is only a minute or two away.

However, there is something very important to be taken into account. Secret aircraft are certainly being built and flown at Nellis. The U2 spy plane was developed and flown there 40 years ago. The Aurora stealth jet was built and test flown there years before it entered service and was admitted by the US government. Indeed sightings of Aurora near Nellis date from about 1982, whereas its existence was not confirmed until nearly a decade later!

I have met and talked with American aviation experts who tell me that there are countless secret aircraft projects at Nellis. As one phrased it, 'These include some things that if you saw them you'd be sure you had seen a spaceship.' They also include, I was told, very sophisticated propulsion systems, 'some revolutionary', for example, nuclear-fuelled motors. He added, 'the aircraft flying there now [1992] will not be known even to most aviation experts until past the year 2000 ... Of course people are seeing amazing things in the sky out there today.' Although he was talking off the record, I have no reason to disbelieve him and the U2, Aurora and other spy-plane technology built in the past at Nellis is common knowledge, not just idle speculation. So something exciting must be under development there now which would amply justify the secrecy.

Indeed, think about it. The US government may be very happy to let wild stories about alien spaceships do the rounds, so much so that they could even be tempted to feed bogus documents to ufologists. It would know how absurd such stories sound to most observers. This just might give them leeway to fly secret aircraft, which, if seen, would be written off as UFOs!

Of course, it then depends upon your views about UFOs.

Either they are nonsense, in which case the sightings are rejected, or else they are true, therefore the sightings are accepted as spaceships. Either way the real source is effectively blurred.

In 1992, Andrew Basiago published some interesting data, said to have been given to a relative by Marion Williams, a former CIA agent who worked for Lockheed aviation. Williams contracted terminal cancer and in his latter days talked about his experiences in Nevada – well before the stories from Lear and Lazar had emerged even to ufologists. He spoke of the facility, its technology to extract data from retrieved spacecraft and even of small details – like being transported there in blacked-out buses – all of which fitted later claims.

However true any of this proves to be, the belief in the importance of the area grows. Film of the UFO called 'Old Faithful'– so regular are its sightings – has entered the UFO scene on several occasions in recent years. It is just a light in the sky.

In April 1993 a UFO conference was held in the town of Rachel near Nellis. Dennis Stacy penned an excellent account in *MUFON Journal* of this event and offered guide-lines to would-be tourists on how to get there and what they might see. Now there are tour buses going there from Las Vegas! On 1 October 1994, Turner Network Television planned a two-hour live show from the Nevada Desert, interspersing pre-recorded interviews on the subject of information and disinformation with any live shots of spaceships they might be lucky enough to get through a very long telephoto lens.

The problem is that the same area attracts aviation freaks. They see the same odd lights as the UFO buffs and go home convinced that they have been watching prototypes of the next generation of stealth technology. The ufologists, of course, agree, but they believe that these craft are modelled on retrieved alien spaceships; and some would even add that they are being test flown by humans under the tutelage of aliens!

It comes down to which version of the truth you believe. Although, if any retrievals have ever happened, nothing is really quite as daft as it seems.

COULD THE SECRET BE KEPT?

If crashed UFOs, alien bodies and, now, working flying saucers have been in the possession of the US government for decades, how could such a mammoth secret have been kept for so long?

All countries have secrets, of course, but usually these emerge after a few years. In the UK, in August 1956, there was a major air crash at a nuclear base in Suffolk. A hangar housing A-bombs caught fire and a catastrophe was only narrowly averted. That truth was withheld from the public for 30 years, but eventually got out when those involved chose to talk.

History shows that huge secrets can be kept with effort. Think of the number of people who worked on the Manhattan Project to build the first atomic bomb. For a couple of years towards the end of World War 2 there were many scientists, technicians and military personnel engaged in the battle to perfect this weapon, and materials were being shipped the length and breadth of the USA without their true purpose being recognized. The world did not learn the truth until the weapon was first used in July 1945.

Perhaps a similar degree of secrecy has been used for retrieved UFOs, the first of which, reputedly, was taken not long after World War 2 ended. The difference is that we are not talking about keeping a secret when the media were held in check, as they were in war-time. Instead, I am suggesting that something as fantastic as crashed spaceships and alien bodies has been the subject of a successful cover-up for 50 years, a period during which the story-hungry media has expanded rapidly, cheque books at the ready. It is, I think, unbelievable to expect that the lid could have been kept on such a secret for such a long time. But, then, even if only some of the incidents in this book are true, the lid has *not* been kept on firmly. This book would not have been written without the co-operation of people who have broken the secret.

Yet, what we have is a secret so potentially incredible that even if it leaked out, most rational people would be disinclined to believe it. The A-bomb story was believed because the weapon was used. However, it is more than probable that, had Japan surrendered before the bomb was used, the Americans would have kept the secret for as long as possible.

By their very nature, secrets are kept secret for a reason; similarly, secrets are unlocked for a reason. As we have seen, there were powerful political, economic and military factors behind the reason for keeping secret the retrieval of alien technology in 1947. Unless things change in the near future – for example, the USA really does have working spaceships flying about or any aliens out there decide to make their presence on earth obvious to all – then there is still no overt reason why that secret should be broken. Indeed, the last thing the authorities would want is the legitimization of UFO study, because it might cause freelance scientists to study it in detail with the potential risk of making breakthroughs before military-controlled scientific teams. This provides a strong motivation not only for hiding the truth, but also for making UFOs seem too absurd to be credible to science. In many ways, the authorities have an excellent ally in this task, in the form of the ufologists themselves, whose over-exuberance and willingness to believe tall stories – without luxuries such as evidence to support them – usually succeeds in making their claims appear very credulous.

Over the years there have been signs that the intelligence community in the USA has sometimes helped to muddy the waters. There is evidence, as we have seen, that it may have helped cast doubt on the Roswell case by seeding a highly dubious retrieval story into the early UFO field. There is plenty to suggest that it had a role in the contactee stories during the 1950s, where witnesses came forward, claiming trips to Mars and Saturn, thus rapidly undermining the fast-accumulating credibility of the subject, particularly as far as the media and mainstream science were concerned.

These days, there are good grounds for believing that dubious documents making extreme claims about alien retrievals are fed to ufologists by official sources, perhaps hoping that ufologists will shoot themselves in the foot by making a big deal out of them; odds on they will.

This all makes no sense if UFOs are unreal or just natural phenomena – however strange. But what if there is some truth behind the alien nature of the phenomenon and the claims that proof of this has been retrieved? No government could hope to hide this news forever. There are always going to be death-bed confessions from scientists, people braving security regulations to 'tell the world the truth' and the occasional official slip-up. So how do you prevent these things from leaking and gradually convincing the world?

Fortunately, this alien truth seems intrinsically absurd, so it will rightly take a lot of swallowing by most rational people, especially without any official confirmation. But if a series of calmly told, consistent and not overly incredulous stories did gradually emerge over the years, it would prove impossible to keep the cork on the bottle.

So what do you do? You help ufologists make their subject appear even more ridiculous than it is. For every step forward that a 'true confession' brings, the UFO buffs will then take two steps backward, thanks to their clearly demonstrated talent for believing anything, no matter how ludicrous, and promptly shouting it from the rooftops. A few dubious-looking documents that express bizarre features of the cover-up, quite conceivably based loosely upon the truth ... The occasional wild story seeded into the UFO community to lead it up the garden path, smelling roses instead of a rat ... If they want to watch secret aircraft from the Nevada Desert and think that they are spaceships, fine – by no means disillusion them ... it is really remarkably simple. Before very long, the UFO movement will strangle itself by making claims so absurd that nobody outside the field believes anything any more. I really think that there is a more than even chance that this is what is going on: disinformation is spread liberally around the subject, but it is not completely *wrong* information, merely an exaggeration of the truth.

I suspect the reality of alien retrievals lies somewhere between the need for belief and disbelief in what is in this book, probably not in alien pacts and spaceships piloted by the USAF, but in the capture of something still incomprehensible and, so, very hot property indeed.

TEXTS OF DOCUMENTS

The originals are reproduced in the photograph section.

DOCUMENT 1
TELETYPE

———

Memo, dated 8 July 1947, in which the FBI discuss the Roswell crash. This follows the reports from Roswell base that the object was a UFO, but precedes by a few hours the claims coming out of Carswell base, in Texas, that the object was merely a weather balloon.

FBI DALLAS   7-8-47   6.17 pm

DIRECTOR AND SAC, CINCINNATI   URGENT

Flying Disc, information concerning. xxxxxxx, headquarters eighth air force, telephonically advised this office that an object purporting to be a flying disc was recovered near Roswell, New Mexico, this date. The disc is hexagonal in shape and was suspended from a balloon by cable, which balloon was approximately twenty feet in diameter. xxxxxxx further advised that the object found resembles a high altitude weather balloon with a radar reflector, but that telephonic conversation between their office and Wright Field had not xxxxxxx borne out this belief. Disc and balloon being transported to Wright Field by special plane for examination. Information provided this office because of national interest in case. xxxxxxx and fact that National Broadcasting Company, Associated Press, and others attempting to break story of location of disc today. xxxxxxx advised would request Wright Field to advise Cincinnati office results of examination. No further investigation being conducted.

END   WYLY RECORDED F B I JUL 22 1947

CXXXX ACK IN ORDER

WA 92 FBI CI MJW

BPI H8

8-38 PM

8-22 PM OK FBI WASH.DC

DOCUMENT 2
OFFICE MEMORANDUM UNITED STATES GOVERNMENT

Released under the US Freedom of Information Act in 1976. It discusses the green fireballs seen over New Mexico in 1948 and shows how seriously these were taken. The name censored is Dr Lincoln La Paz, whose association with the Roswell crash is controversial.

TO   : DIRECTOR, FBI   Date: March 22 1949
FROM   : SAC, SAN ANTONIO
SUBJECT : PROTECTION OF VITAL INSTALLATIONS BUREAU FILE 65-58300

Re San Antonio letter dated January 31, 1949, which outlined discussion had at recent weekly Intelligence Conference of G-2, ONI, OSI and FBI in the Fourth Army Area concerning 'Unidentified Aircraft' or 'Unidentified Aerial Phenomena' otherwise known as 'flying discs', 'flying saucers' and 'balls of fire'. It is repeated that this matter is considered secret by intelligence officers of both the Army and the Air Force.

G–2, 4th Army, has now advised that the above matter is now termed 'Unconventional Aircraft' and investigations concerning such matters have been given the name 'Project Grudge'.

G–2, 4th Army, advised on February 16, 1949, a conference was held at Los Alamos, New Mexico, to consider the so-called 'Green fire ball phenomena' which began about December 5, 1948. It was brought out this question has been classified 'secret' and that investigation is now the primary responsibility of the US Air Force, Air Material Command, T–2.

xxxxxxx of the University of New Mexico, discussed one siting which he himself had made which was termed the 'Starvation Peak incident' and described the following characteristics which indicated that the phenomenon could not be classified as a normal meteorite fall.

1. There was an initial bright light (no period of intensity increase) and constant intensity during the duration of the phenomenon.
2. Yellow green color about 5200 Angstroms.
3. Essentially horizontal path.
4. Trajectory traversed at constant angular velocity.
5. Duration about two seconds.
6. No accompanying noise.

DOCUMENT 3
AERIAL PHENOMENA ENQUIRY NETWORK

---

*A part of the report sent to me in 1975 by the mysterious, anonymous
APEN. At the time, nobody suspected that the Llandrillo affair covered
up a landing by an alien craft. It was almost 20 years before eyewitness
testimony about this event surfaced.*

COPY OF INITIAL REPORT CONCERNING NORTH WALES
    LANDING. TRANSMITTED 24 JAN 74
UFO
PRIORY
VIA T/P LINK 03
PRIORITY ONE RELEASE AUTHORIZATION JTA
TO REFERENCE CENTRE
FM: AGENTS 71 & 349
CASE No 174L.74.71/349ST

LOCALITY:- LLANxxxxxx NORTH WALES
INCIDENT:- LANDING AND CONTACT (ALMOST PROVEN)
RECOMMENDED ACTION:- 'TIME REGRESSION' HYPNOSIS
    (ASAP)
DESCRIPTION OF OBJECT:- DISCOID, DOMED, BALL & TRIPOD
    UNDERCARRIAGE, 4 PORTHOLES
SIZE:- 200' x 50'
COLOUR:- METALLIC (POLISHED)

EXTRA EQUIPT NEEDED:- LAND ROVER, LWB, THEOF-
    DOLOITE, STROBOSCOPE, INFRA RED / ULTRA VIOLET
    SENSORS, WALKIE TALKIES (5)
AT WHAT DATE NEEDED:- TOMORROW (25 JAN 74)
NUMBER OF EXTRA PERSONNEL NEEDED:- 4 (RECOMMEND
    AT LEAST ONE BE FEMALE)
ANY OTHER COMMENTS:- REQUEST NEW ISSUE OF INITIAL
    REPORT FORMS BE DELIVERED TO MY HOME ADDRESS
    AND THAT OF AGENT 349

Having interviewed Mr Wxxxxxxx at length (2½ hours) as instructed.
We found him to be very sincere. He was unshakable as far as his
story is concerned and his description of the craft (and aliens) was
more detailed than that to which we have become accustomed, perhaps this is because he is an ex-soldier/engineer. He described a typical 'Adamski' Scout Ship with a few 'extra' details. His description

of the Aliens was also reminiscent of Adamski's Aliens. The craft description was similar to the Lake District report and also the Rossendale Valley area report (summer 1972). The Aliens are said to have spoken to him, given him instructions to contact us only and also furnished him with one of our X-D nos.

DOCUMENT 4
UNCLASSIFIED

Typical of the UFO files released by the MoD in the UK since early 1983. This one describes a sighting by Yorkshire police officers on 16 August 1987. The distribution list is the most interesting piece of information. Copies go to DI 55 (a defence intelligence agency) and two copies to DSTI (a science and technology unit, possibly at RAF Farnborough). These departments have never released details.

CYO225 17/1936 229C2391

FOR CAB
ROUTINE 171400Z AUG 87

FROM RAF WEST DRAYTON
TO MODUK AIR

U N C L A S S I F I E D
SIC X6F
SUBJECT: AERIAL PHENOMENA A.161900Z AUG 87, 30 SECS B.ONE, DARK ROUND OBJECT, NO LIGHTS, NO SOUND C. AT HOME ADDRESS - OUTDOORS - STATIONARY D. NAKED EYE E. TO THE SOUTH OF PINNER F. 45 DEGREES WHEN SIGHTED PASSING TO OVERHEAD G. N/K H. STEADY SOUTH - NORTH J. CLEAR/CAVOK K. RESIDENTIAL AREA L. WATCH MANAGERS DESK LATCC M. xxxxxxx

O. NIL P. 171230Z AUG 87
BT

DISTRIBUTION Z6F
F
CAB 1 Sec (AS) ACTION (CXJ 1)
CYD 1 DD GE/AEW
CAV 1 DI 55
CAV 2 DSTI

DOCUMENT 5
MINISTRY OF DEFENCE
Defence Secretariat Division 8

---

*The first breakthrough in the Rendlesham Forest case in the UK. After
two years of denials, the MoD confirmed to me, on 13 April 1983, that
the event had occurred. This was the MoD's first-ever admission in
public that it had unsolved landing cases on file.*

Main Building   Whitehall   London SW1A 2HB

Miss J Randles   Our reference D/DS8/10/209
xxxxxxxxxxxxxxx   Date   13 April 1983

Dear Miss Randles,

Thank you for your recent correspondence on the subject of UFOs.

As regards your offer to summarise the reports held by this
Department there really is very little to summarise. I attach a copy of
a blank report form showing the type of information we require
together with a couple of examples of completed reports (with the
name and address of the informant deleted for reasons of confidentiality). I am sure you will agree that, although we hold a large number of reports, each one is indeed very brief.

Turning now to your interest in the sighting at RAF Woodbridge in
December 1980, I can confirm that USAF personnel did see unusual
lights outside the boundary fence early in the morning of 27 December
1980 but no explanation for the occurrence was ever forthcoming.
There is, however, no question of the account being a cover-up for a
crashed aircraft or testing of secret devices as you suggest, nor was
there any contact with 'alien beings'.

I understand that an article on the Woodbridge sighting has been
published in the magazine 'OMNI' (Vol 5 No 6) in which you may be
interested.

Yours sincerely,

PJ Titchmarsh (Mrs)

DOCUMENT 6
DEPARTMENT OF THE AIR FORCE

———

The famous Halt memorandum, in which RAF Bentwater's commander, Charles Halt, reports the Rendlesham Forest case. This was denied by the British government to the Guardian *newspaper even eight months after its release in 1983 under the US Freedom of Information Act.*

REPLY TO:
ATTN OF: CD   13 Jan 81
SUBJECT: Unexplained Lights
TO: RAF/CC

1. Early in the morning of 27 Dec 80 (approximately 0300L), two USAF security police patrolmen saw unusual lights outside the back gate at RAF Woodbridge. Thinking an aircraft might have crashed or been forced down, they called for permission to go outside the gate to investigate. The on-duty flight chief responded and allowed three patrolmen to proceed on foot. The individuals reported seeing a strange glowing object in the forest. The object was described as being metalic in appearance and triangular in shape, approximately two to three meters across the base and approximately two meters high. It illuminated the entire forest with a white light. The object itself had a pulsing red light on top and a bank(s) of blue lights underneath. The object was hovering or on legs. As the patrolmen approached the object, it maneuvered through the trees and disappeared. At this time the animals on a nearby farm went into a frenzy. The object was briefly sighted approximately an hour later near the back gate.

2. The next day, three depressions 1½" deep and 7" in diameter were found where the object had been sighted on the ground. The following night (29 Dec 80) the area was checked for radiation. Beta/gamma readings of 0.1 milliroentgens were recorded with peak readings in the three depressions and near the center of the triangle formed by the depressions. A nearby tree had moderate (.05-.07) readings on the side of the tree toward the depressions.

3. Later in the night a red sun-like light was seen through the trees. It moved about and pulsed. At one point it appeared to throw off glowing particles and then broke into five separate white objects and then disappeared. Immediately thereafter, three star-like objects were noticed in the sky, two objects to the north and one to the south, all

of which were about 10° off the horizon. The objects moved rapidly in sharp angular movements and displayed red, green and blue lights. The objects to the north appeared to be elliptical through an 8-12 power lens. They then turned to full circles. The objects to the north remained in the sky for an hour or more. The object to the south was visible for two or three hours and beamed down a stream of light from time to time. Numerous individuals, including the undersigned, witnessed the activities in paragraphs 2 and 3.

CHARLES I. HALT, Lt Col. USAF
Deputy Base Commander

DOCUMENT 7

One of the documents released by the US FoI Act about the mysterious project 'Moon Dust'. This clearly links it with UFOs, although it is widely considered to be connected with the retrieval of debris from space.

I170060080

Country: MOROCCO	IR MF Roll: 1439
Subject: UFO sighting at Kasba Tadla, Morocco (32° 36' N 06° 17' W) (U)	Rpt: 1 865 0069 67
	DR: 6 April 1967
DI: 28 March 1967	No pages: 1
Pl & Date Acq: Rabat, Morocco 2 April 1967	Ref: Project MOON DUST
	Originator: USDAO Rabat,
Eval: C-3	Morocco
Source: Local Press	Prep by:
Info Spec: ENS/1s	
Distr: BXP	Appr Auth: C G STRUM, CAPT, USN UN DEFENSE ATTACHE, RABAT

Extract of Report

1. this report forwards a translation of an article which appeared in the Petit Morocain, 2 April 1967. This item was not carried in the other daily newspapers, but is significant as it indicates continued local interest in the subject of UFOs.

REFERENCES

Chapter 1

1871

An Account of a Meeting with Denizens of Another World, Langford, D. (David & Charles, 1979/St Martin's Press, 1980)
UFO Brigantia (July 1990)

1884

The Emergence of a Phenomenon, Clark, J. (Omnigraphics, 1992): pp. 107–8

1897

'Aurora Spaceman – RIP?', Buckle, E. (*FSR*, vol. 19, no. 4, 1973)
'The UFO crash of 1897', Hewes, H. (*Official UFO*), January 1976, Clark, J., op. cit.: pp. 110–12

1908

UFOs from Behind the Iron Curtain, Hobana, I. and Weverbergh, J. (Souvenir, 1974): Chapter 1
The Fire Came By, Baxter, J. and Atkins, T. (Doubleday, 1976)
'The Nuclear Explosion that Shook the Earth', Zabawski, W. (*Official UFO*, November 1976 and May 1977)
'Interview with Dr James Van Allen', Randle, K. and Cornett, R.C. (*UFO Quest*, issue 1, 1977)
Chekhov's Journey, Watson, I. (Gollancz, 1981)

1925

Letter from the witness to me (4 June 1990)

1946

Genesis, Harbinson, W. (Corgi, 1980)
'Project 1946', Liljegren, A. (*AFU*, 1985)
'The Ghost Rockets', Liljegren, A. and Svahn, C. in *UFOs 47–87,* edited by Evans, H. and Spencer, J. (Fortean Times, 1987)
Greenwood, B. in various issues of *Just Cause*
The Complete Book of UFOs, Hough, P. and Randles, J. (Piatkus, 1994)

Chapter 2

Roswell

Stringfield, L., status reports on witnesses in *FSR*, vol. 25, no. 4 (1979); 25, no. 6 (1980); and 28, no. 3 (1983)
Moore, W. (with Berlitz, C.) *The Roswell Incident* (Grafton, 1980)
— Proceedings of the MUFON Conference, 1982 (MUFON)
— (with others) *Focus* (Sept and Dec 1990, Mar 1991)
MUFON Journal (Sept 1990)
Randle, K. and Schmitt, D. in *International UFO Reporter* Nov 1989, Mar and Nov 1990, Jul 1991, May 1993, Jan 1994
— *MUFON Journal* (Apr 1991)
— *UFO Crash at Roswell* (Avon Books, 1991)
— *The Truth About the UFO Crash at Roswell* (M. Evans, 1994)
Schaffner, R. on V-2 theory, *UFO Brigantia* (Summer 1989)
Rodeghier, M. on-site analysis, *International UFO Reporter* (Sept 1989, Nov 1990)
Carey, T. on archaeologists debate, *International UFO Reporter* (Nov 1991, Nov 1993, Jan 1994); see also 'The Roswell Report' CUFOS (1991)
The plains of San Agustin controversy CUFOS and FUFOR (1992)
Allan C. (Dr La Paz), *Orbiter* (Jul 1991)
International UFO Reporter (May 1993)
Fisher, P., Marcell jnr interview, *MUFON Journal* (Jul 1991)
Crash at Corona, Friedman, S. and Berliner, D. (Paragon House, 1992)
Klass, P. on GAO inquiry, *Skeptics UFO Newsletter,* Jan, Mar and May 1994; see also Rodeghier, M. in *International UFO Reporter,* Mar 1994

Chapter 3

Aztec

Behind the Flying Saucers, Scully, F. (Holt, 1950)

Stringfield, L. status reports in *FSR*, vol. 25, no. 5 (1980) and 28, no. 4 (1983)

MJ–2 and the Riddle of Hangar 18, Beckley, T. (Inner Light, 1989)

James, W. and Minshall, R. in *International UFO Reporter* (Sept 1991)

Laredo

Stringfield, L. status reports in *FSR* vol. 25, no. 4, 1979

Beckley, T. (1989), op. cit.: pp. 70–90

Chapter 4

1952

Harbinson (1980), op. cit.

Moore, W. *Focus* (Dec 1990)

Braenne, O. J. *UFO Brigantia*, 51 and 52 (1992), plus lecture to the IUN Conference, Sheffield (August 1993)

1953

Stringfield, L. status reports in *FSR*, vol. 25, no. 4 (1979); 25, no. 5 (1980); 28, no. 2 (1982)

Moore, W. in 'MUFON Proceedings, 1982', op. cit.

1955

La Fontaine, J. in *UFO Universe* (Aug 1991)

Ubutuba

APRO Bulletin (Mar and May 1960)

UFOs? Yes!, Saunders, D. and Harkins, R. (Ward, 1968)

Craig, R., 'Physical Evidence' in *Scientific Study of UFOs*, edited by Condon, E. (Bantam, 1969)

Encyclopedia of UFOs, edited by Story, R. (New English Library, 1980)

Chalker, W. various private communications

Silpho

Private archives of Dr J. Dale, shown to author (1988)

Randles, J. in *UFO Brigantia* (Nov 1988)

Ford, R. in *UFO Debate* (1990)

1959

Hobana and Weverbergh (1974), op. cit.: pp. 1–2

Chapter 5

1961

Michaels, W. in *Ideal UFO* (8, 1979)

Demidov, V. in Beckley (1989), op. cit.

1963

Various contemporary newspapers, as cited

FSR vol. 9. no. 5 and 9, no. 6 (1963)

Fuller, P. in *The Crop Watcher* (Sept 1992)

Cosford

Wolverhampton Express & Star (7 Jan 1964)

FSR, vol 10, nos 2, 3 and 4 (1964)

Private interview and correspondence, as cited

Holloman

UFOs: Past, Present & Future, Emenegger, R. (Ballantine, 1974)

Private correspondence, as cited

Fort Riley

Stringfield, L. status reports in *FSR*, vol. 25, no. 6 (1980) and 28, no. 3 (1983)

'In Search of a UFO Stereotype', Randles, J. and Dillon, W. in *FSR* vol. 28, no. 4 (1983)

Rogue River, Oregon, file, 'Project Blue Book' archives

Argentina

FSR, vol. 11, no. 3 (1965)

Kecksburg

Sanderson, I. in *Fate* (Mar 1966)

Stringfield, L. status report in *FSR*, vol. 28, no. 4 (1983)

Various letters and retrieved files, thanks to Boeche, R. in 1984

Acme, Pennsylvania, meteor, 'Project Blue Book' archives

Updates (e.g. from Gordon, S.) in *MUFON Journal*, Feb, Sept and Oct 1989; Feb 1991

1967

Assorted contemporary Press coverage, as cited

Chapter 6
1974

Pace, A. in *BUFORA Journal* (Spring 1974)

Buckle, E. in *FSR* (Case Histories 18, 1974)

Earthlights, Devereux, P. (Turnstone Press, 1982)

'The Mystery of APEN', Randles, J. in *The Unknown*, Jul, Aug and Sept 1986)

Fry, M. personal interviews (1993)

1977

Chiumeiento, A. in *FSR*, vol. 30, no. 2 (1985)

1979

Pennine UFO Mystery, Randles, J. (Grafton, 1983)

Assorted personal interviews and correspondence, as cited

Chapter 7
1980

Randles, J. in *FSR*, vol. 26, no. 6 (1981) and vol. 27, no. 6 (1982)

Randles, J. in *The Unexplained* (Orbis partwork, 1982)

Mischera, E. in *OMNI* (Feb 1983)

Sky Crash, Butler, B., Street, D. and Randles, J. (Spearman, 1984; updated, Grafton, 1986)

From Out of the Blue, Randles, J. (Inner Light, 1991; updated Berkley, 1993)

Boeche, R., Randles, J. and Huneeus, A. in *Fate* (Sept 1993)

Plus numerous files, documents, interviews and correspondence

1984

Stringfield, L. in *MUFON Journal* (Feb 1989)

1986

Private information

1989

Sceptical appraisal in *UFO Brigantia* (May 1989)

'Summary of Quest story', Huneeus, A. in *UFO Universe* (Jul 1990)

Investigation by Hinde, C. in *UFO Times* (BUFORA), May 1993

Chapter 8
1991

World UFO Journal (4, 1993)

Oeschler, B. in *UFO Library* (Oct and Dec 1993)

1993

Private information (by word of mouth only – so far!)

Chapter 9

For details on the cover-up and data on alien autopsies, Area 51, etc., see:

FSR, vol. 25, no. 6 (1980); 28, no. 2 (1982); 28, no. 3 (1983); 31, no. 5 (1986)

UFO Brigantia (May 1989)

UFO Universe (Jan and July 1990, February 1991, Spring 1992)

MUFON Journal (Jul 1992, June, Aug and Oct 1993)

International UFO Reporter (Sept 1990, Sept 1991)

Oeschler, B. interview in *Strange Days* (1, 1994)

ADDRESSES

The following publications are cited in the text: *APRO Bulletin, Focus, Ideal UFO, Official UFO, UFO Brigantia, UFO Debate, UFO Quest* and *The Unknown*. However, they appear now to be defunct. You may find old copies via the cited specialist mail-order bookfinders, who will also be useful for older UFO titles. *The Unexplained* (part-work) has since been republished under several titles, in hardback and paperback form, by Orbis. Other existing publishers are:

AFU, PO Box 11027, S–60011 Norrkoping, Sweden

Crop Watcher, 3 Selbourne Court, Tavistock Close, Romsey, Hampshire so51 7TY, UK

Fate, Box 1940, 170 Future Way, Marion, OH 43305–1940, USA

FSR, FSR Publications, Snodland, Kent ME6 5HJ, UK

International UFO Reporter, 2457 West Peterson Ave, Chicago, IL 60659, USA

Just Cause, Box 218, Coventry, CT 06238, USA

MUFON UFO Journal, 103 Oldtowne Road, Seguin, TX 78155–4099, USA

Orbiter, Box 652, Reading, MA 01867, USA

Quest, Grassington, N.Yorkshire, UK.

Skeptics UFO Newsletter, 560 N Street SW, Washington DC 20024, USA

Strange Days, 9 Broderick Close, Kenton Bar, Newcastle upon Tyne NE3 3SG, UK

UFO Afrinews, PO Box MP 49, Mount Pleasant, Harare, Zimbabwe

UFO Library, PO Box 461116, Escondido, CA 92046–9892, USA

UFO Universe, 11 East 30th Street, Suite 4R, New York, NY 10016, USA

World UFO Journal, 16 Newton Green, Great Dunmow, Essex CM6 1DU, UK

Books and magazines are available by mail order via:

Arcturus, 1443 SE Port St Lucie Boulevard, Port St Lucie, FL 34952, USA

Midnight Books, The Mount, Ascerton Road, Sidmouth, Devon EX10 9BT, UK

Specialist Knowledge, 20 Paul Street, Frome, Somerset, BA11 1DX, UK
Sydney Esoteric, 475–9 Elizabeth Street, Surry Hills, NSW 2010,
  Australia

The J. Allen Hynek Center for UFO Studies is strongly recommended
as an objective and skilled scientific research group. Contact it via
the *International UFO Reporter* address above.

MUFON (Mutual UFO Network) is the world's largest membership
association. Contact it via the *MUFON Journal* address above.

CAUS (Citizens Against UFO Secrecy) adopts a commonsense
approach to document retrieval. Contact it via the *Just Cause* address
above.

In the UK, the leading membership group is BUFORA (British UFO
Research Association), c/o Suite 1, 2c Leyton Road, Harpenden,
Hertfordshire AL5 2TL.

Alien Acknowledgment Campaign (AAC), an association fighting
UFO secrecy, was formed in 1993. Contact it: c/o 20 Newton Gardens,
Ripon, N. Yorkshire HG4 1QF.

UFO Call is a weekly information service updating all current news.
Available (UK only) and, as of summer 1994, written and recorded by
Jenny Randles for BUFORA: (tel: 01891) 121886.

In June 1994 a bold venture, *The New UFOlogist*, was launched by
leading European ufologists. This is the world's first non-profit-
making, fully independent, UFO publication, with a very objective
approach to the evidence. It aims to put each issue together by way
of a unique, open forum to which all comers are invited to help decide
content and assign commissions. All money raised will go into a central fund – again openly administered by all who wish to join – and
to which anyone can submit proposals for research programmes and
case investigations that require more detailed work. The research will
remain the property of the individual concerned, but *The New
UFOlogist* has first publications rights on it. Contact the publication
at: 71 Knight Avenue, Canterbury, Kent CT2 5PY, UK.

Readers can pass information to the author (in full confidence, if
required) at: 11 Pike Court, Fleetwood, Lancashire FY7 8QF, UK.

INDEX